The Art of Breaking: Mastering Reverse Engineering Techniques

Isidore Eichenbaum

Welcome to the intriguing realm of reverse engineering, where the seemingly impenetrable becomes a puzzle waiting to be solved. **"The Art of Breaking: Mastering Reverse Engineering Techniques"** is your guide to unraveling the secrets hidden within software, hardware, and networks. In the following pages, we embark on a journey through the intricate world of reverse engineering, a discipline that empowers individuals to dissect, understand, and even manipulate the very fabric of technology.

Defining the Art

Reverse engineering is more than just a set of technical skills; it is an art form that requires a curious mind, a keen eye for detail, and a passion for unraveling complexity. In this book, we delve into the core of this art, exploring its origins, applications, and the transformative power it holds. Whether you are a seasoned professional seeking to enhance your skills or a curious enthusiast looking to enter this captivating field, this book serves as your comprehensive guide.

A Journey Through History

As we embark on this journey, we take a moment to trace the historical evolution of reverse engineering. From its humble beginnings to its pivotal role in modern technology, we uncover the pivotal moments and pioneers that have shaped the discipline. Understanding the roots of reverse engineering provides a context for appreciating its significance in today's ever-evolving technological landscape.

Applications Across Industries

Reverse engineering is not confined to a single industry; its applications span a vast spectrum. Whether it's breaking down software barriers, unraveling the secrets of hardware, or deciphering intricate network protocols, the art finds its place in diverse domains. We explore the multifaceted applications of reverse engineering, demonstrating its relevance in cybersecurity, software development, hardware design, and beyond.

Throughout this book, we aim to equip you with the knowledge, tools, and techniques needed to master the art of breaking. Each chapter is crafted to build upon the last, guiding you through the fundamentals, advanced methodologies, and ethical considerations that define the landscape of reverse engineering.

So, let the journey begin. Unleash your curiosity, sharpen your analytical skills, and join us in mastering the art of breaking.

1. Introduction to Reverse Engineering

Welcome to the captivating world of reverse engineering—a realm where the curious mind becomes a digital detective, dissecting the intricacies of technology. In this introductory chapter, we embark on a journey to define the essence of reverse engineering, transcending it beyond a mere technical skill and portraying it as an art form. Discover the power that lies in unraveling the mysteries of software, hardware, and networks, and understand the profound impact it has on industries ranging from cybersecurity to software development. Whether you're a seasoned practitioner seeking to deepen your understanding or a curious enthusiast stepping into this fascinating field, this chapter lays the groundwork for an exploration into the heart of reverse engineering.

1.1 The Definition and Purpose of Reverse Engineering

Reverse engineering, a captivating discipline within the realm of technology, encapsulates a nuanced art of unraveling, decoding, and understanding complex systems. At its core, reverse engineering is the process of dissecting a technology or system to unveil its internal workings, design principles, and functionalities. Unlike traditional engineering, which involves creating something new, reverse engineering involves breaking down and analyzing an existing structure. This multifaceted practice serves a myriad of purposes, ranging from troubleshooting and innovation to security and compliance.

The primary goal of reverse engineering is to comprehend the inner workings of a technology or system that may not be readily accessible through conventional means. By peeling back the layers, a reverse engineer seeks to understand the intricacies of software, hardware, or any complex system, often in situations where documentation or source code is not available. This process enables practitioners to gain insights into the underlying algorithms, protocols, and structures, fostering a deeper understanding of how a system operates.

One of the fundamental purposes of reverse engineering lies in troubleshooting and problem-solving. When faced with malfunctioning software or hardware, engineers employ reverse engineering techniques to identify and rectify issues. This involves deconstructing the components, tracing the flow of data, and pinpointing where errors or inefficiencies occur. Through this process, engineers can develop targeted solutions, enhancing the reliability and performance of the system.

Innovation is another key driver behind the practice of reverse engineering. By dissecting existing technologies, engineers can glean inspiration, discover novel design patterns, and identify opportunities for improvement. This aspect is particularly evident in industries where rapid advancements are essential, such as consumer electronics and software development. Reverse engineering empowers innovators to build upon existing foundations, creating products that push the boundaries of what is possible.

Security is a critical facet of reverse engineering, particularly in the realm of cybersecurity. Reverse engineers play a pivotal role in assessing the security of software, identifying vulnerabilities, and developing countermeasures. This proactive approach allows security experts to stay one step ahead of potential threats, ensuring the integrity of systems and protecting against malicious exploits. Understanding the inner workings of malware through reverse engineering is equally essential for developing effective antivirus solutions and mitigating cyber threats.

Compliance and interoperability are additional areas where reverse engineering proves indispensable. In industries governed by strict standards or proprietary technologies, reverse engineering can be employed to ensure compliance with regulations. Moreover, when integrating diverse systems that may not inherently communicate with each other, reverse engineering aids in deciphering communication protocols, fostering interoperability, and facilitating seamless interaction between disparate technologies.

Reverse engineering is not confined to the digital domain; it extends its reach into the physical realm, particularly in the field of hardware. When dealing with legacy systems, obsolete components, or unsupported hardware, reverse engineering becomes a lifeline. Engineers can analyze and recreate components, ensuring the continued operation of critical infrastructure even when original parts are no longer available.

The methodology of reverse engineering encompasses various techniques and tools, each tailored to the nature of the system under investigation. In software reverse engineering, disassemblers and decompilers play a crucial role, allowing analysts to inspect and comprehend machine-level code. Hardware reverse engineering, on the other hand, involves techniques such as circuit analysis and firmware extraction to decipher the inner workings of electronic devices.

Despite its manifold benefits, reverse engineering is not without challenges and ethical considerations. Intellectual property concerns often surround the practice, especially when applied to proprietary software or patented hardware. Striking a balance between innovation and protecting the rights of original creators is a delicate dance in the landscape of reverse engineering. Ethical considerations also come into play when dealing with sensitive information, and responsible disclosure practices are vital to maintaining ethical standards within the field.

In conclusion, the definition and purpose of reverse engineering unfold as a dynamic and indispensable practice within the technological panorama. It serves as a gateway to understanding, troubleshooting, innovating, securing, and ensuring the compliance and interoperability of complex systems. As technology continues to evolve, so too will the significance of reverse engineering, guiding us through the intricate pathways of discovery and innovation in the ever-expanding digital landscape.

1.2 A Brief History of Reverse Engineering

The roots of reverse engineering extend deep into the annals of technological evolution, weaving a narrative of innovation, necessity, and adaptation. A journey through the brief history of reverse engineering unveils a trajectory marked by ingenuity and a relentless pursuit of understanding complex systems.

The origins of reverse engineering can be traced back to the early days of computing, a time when the boundaries of technology were continually being pushed. In the mid-20th century, during the advent of mainframe computers, engineers and programmers were confronted with the challenge of comprehending and modifying software that lacked the luxury of user-friendly interfaces. In this nascent era, reverse engineering emerged as a pragmatic response to the need for understanding machine code and deciphering the functionalities of software.

One of the early applications of reverse engineering was in the realm of software compatibility. As computing systems diversified, software developers faced the challenge of creating programs that could run on multiple platforms. Reverse engineering allowed them to examine the binary code of software designed for a specific system, understand its functionality, and adapt it to run on different architectures. This marked the genesis of a practice that would later become indispensable in fostering interoperability.

The proliferation of proprietary software in the latter half of the 20th century spurred the evolution of reverse engineering. As companies guarded their source code and algorithms as closely held secrets, reverse engineers took on the challenge of deciphering these concealed systems. This was not always driven by malicious intent; in many instances, engineers sought to understand proprietary technologies to create compatible products or improve upon existing designs.

The video game industry witnessed a significant chapter in the history of reverse engineering during the 1980s and 1990s. Copy protection mechanisms implemented by game developers prompted enthusiasts to engage in reverse engineering to circumvent these protections. This practice, often driven by the desire to create backup copies of games or enable interoperability, sparked debates around copyright infringement and fair use.

The advent of personal computing in the 1980s and the democratization of technology gave rise to a new wave of reverse engineering. Software applications, both commercial and open-source, became more accessible to a broader audience. This accessibility, coupled with a growing community of enthusiasts, led to the development of tools and methodologies that facilitated reverse engineering. The emergence of disassemblers, debuggers, and decompilers marked a turning point, empowering individuals to delve into the intricacies of binary code.

The legal landscape surrounding reverse engineering has witnessed notable developments over the years. Landmark cases, such as the 1992 case Sega v. Accolade in the United States, set important precedents regarding the legality of reverse engineering for interoperability purposes. These legal battles underscored the delicate balance between protecting intellectual property and fostering innovation through reverse engineering.

In the realm of cybersecurity, the history of reverse engineering takes on a critical dimension. Security experts and ethical hackers have employed reverse engineering techniques to analyze malware, identify vulnerabilities, and fortify systems against cyber threats. The constant cat-and-mouse game between cyber attackers and defenders has elevated reverse engineering to a crucial tool in the arsenal of cybersecurity professionals.

The 21st century has seen reverse engineering become an integral part of technological innovation. Open-source software, collaborative development, and a culture of information sharing have led to a more transparent approach. Ethical considerations and responsible disclosure practices have become pillars of the modern reverse engineering community, emphasizing the importance of legal and ethical standards in the pursuit of understanding and improving technology.

As we stand on the precipice of an era dominated by artificial intelligence, the Internet of Things, and ever-evolving digital landscapes, the history of reverse engineering serves as a compass guiding us through the complexities of innovation. From its humble beginnings as a necessity-driven practice to its current status as a dynamic force in cybersecurity and technological advancement, reverse engineering continues to shape the way we interact with and understand the intricate machinery of the digital world.

1.3 Applications and Industries

The applications of reverse engineering span a vast and diverse landscape, influencing numerous industries and playing a pivotal role in technological advancement. From troubleshooting and innovation to security and compliance, the versatile nature of reverse engineering finds relevance in a myriad of contexts, shaping the way industries evolve and adapt to the ever-changing technological landscape.

1. Aerospace and Defense:

The aerospace and defense industry has been a longstanding beneficiary of reverse engineering. In this sector, the analysis of existing components, such as aircraft parts or military hardware, allows engineers to understand design principles, enhance performance, and create compatible replacements. Reverse engineering is instrumental in modernizing legacy systems, ensuring they meet contemporary standards without compromising interoperability.

2. Automotive:

In the automotive industry, reverse engineering plays a crucial role in product development and innovation. Companies may reverse engineer competitor vehicles to understand design choices, improve upon existing features, and enhance performance. Additionally, reverse engineering is employed in the aftermarket sector to create compatible replacement parts, contributing to the maintenance and repair of vehicles.

3. Consumer Electronics:

The rapid pace of innovation in consumer electronics necessitates a deep understanding of existing technologies. Reverse engineering enables companies to analyze competitors' devices, explore novel design patterns, and enhance functionalities. This is particularly evident in the smartphone industry, where manufacturers strive to create cutting-edge devices by leveraging insights gained through reverse engineering.

4. Software Development:

In the realm of software development, reverse engineering is employed for various purposes. Developers may reverse engineer legacy software to understand its functionality and ensure compatibility with newer systems. Additionally, the analysis of third-party software or proprietary algorithms aids in creating interoperable solutions, contributing to a more connected and collaborative software ecosystem.

5. Cybersecurity:

The fight against cyber threats relies heavily on reverse engineering. Cybersecurity professionals use reverse engineering to analyze malware, identify vulnerabilities in software, and understand the tactics employed by cybercriminals. By dissecting malicious code, security experts can develop effective countermeasures and fortify systems against potential attacks.

6. Medical Devices:

In the medical field, reverse engineering is employed to understand and improve upon existing medical devices. This is particularly crucial in cases where manufacturers may no longer support a specific device or when creating compatible components for older systems. Reverse engineering contributes to the maintenance and enhancement of medical equipment, ensuring its continued efficacy.

7. Architecture and Archaeology:

Beyond the traditional realms of technology, reverse engineering finds applications in architecture and archaeology. In architecture, historical buildings or structures may be reverse engineered to understand construction methods, materials used, and architectural principles. Similarly, in archaeology, artifacts can be meticulously analyzed through reverse engineering techniques to uncover details about their origin, purpose, and construction.

8. Gaming Industry:

The gaming industry has witnessed extensive use of reverse engineering, particularly in the context of video game development. Game developers may reverse engineer existing games to understand gameplay mechanics, graphics rendering techniques, and innovative features. This knowledge contributes to the creation of new and engaging gaming experiences.

9. Legal and Forensic Investigations:

In the legal and forensic domains, reverse engineering is employed to investigate intellectual property disputes, patent infringements, and other legal matters. Forensic experts may use reverse engineering to analyze digital evidence, reconstruct digital incidents, and gain insights into the methods used in cybercrimes.

10. Environmental Conservation:

In environmental science, reverse engineering techniques can be applied to understand complex ecosystems, model environmental processes, and analyze the impact of human activities on natural systems. This holistic approach contributes to informed decision-making in environmental conservation efforts.

As technology continues to advance, the applications of reverse engineering will likely expand into new frontiers, shaping industries that are yet to emerge. Its role as a catalyst for innovation, problem-solving, and adaptability underscores its significance in the ever-evolving landscape of technology and industry.

2. Fundamentals of Binary Analysis

In this chapter, we dive into the foundational principles that underpin the art of reverse engineering— the fundamentals of binary analysis. Binary code, the language of computers, conceals a wealth of information waiting to be deciphered. We start by unraveling the basics, exploring the anatomy of binary code and understanding the intricate dance of ones and zeros that form the backbone of software. As we venture deeper, we demystify the techniques of disassembling code, equipping you with the skills to break down complex programs into a language that is both understandable and manipulable. Decompilation becomes a powerful tool in our arsenal, allowing us to traverse the realm of assembly language instructions and gain insights into the inner workings of executable files. Join us as we lay the groundwork for your journey into mastering binary analysis, unlocking the gateways to a world where code speaks, and understanding is the key.

2.1 Understanding Binary Code Basics

In the vast realm of reverse engineering, a fundamental cornerstone is laid upon the comprehension of binary code basics. Binary code, the fundamental language of computers, operates at the core of software and firmware, encapsulating a series of zeros and ones that orchestrate the intricate dance of computation. In this section, we embark on a journey to unravel the essence of binary code, exploring its structure, significance, and the pivotal role it plays in the digital world.

Binary Code Unveiled:

At its essence, binary code represents a system of encoding information using only two symbols: 0 and 1. Each binary digit, or bit, is a basic unit of information, analogous to a switch that can be in one of two states—either on (1) or off (0). These binary digits, when organized into groups, form bytes, which serve as the building blocks for encoding information in a computer system.

Numeric Representation:

In the binary system, numbers are represented using only the digits 0 and 1. Unlike the familiar decimal system, which utilizes ten digits (0-9), the binary system uses a base-2 representation. Each digit in a binary number represents a power of 2, starting from the rightmost digit. For example, the binary number 1011 is equivalent to $(1 * 2^3) + (0 * 2^2) + (1 * 2^1) + (1 * 2^0)$ in decimal notation.

ASCII and Character Representation:

Beyond numbers, binary code is employed to represent characters using the ASCII (American Standard Code for Information Interchange) encoding. Each character is assigned a unique binary code, allowing computers to interpret and display a wide range of symbols, letters, and numbers. For instance, the ASCII code for the letter 'A' is represented as 01000001 in binary.

Binary Arithmetic:

Understanding binary arithmetic is fundamental in decoding the operations performed by a computer's central processing unit (CPU). Addition, subtraction, multiplication, and division in the binary system follow principles similar to those in the decimal system but with only two digits (0 and 1). Binary addition involves carrying over to the next digit when the sum exceeds 1, similar to carrying over in decimal addition.

Binary and Memory Storage:

Binary code also plays a pivotal role in memory storage within computers. The binary digits are organized into bytes, and these bytes are used to represent data in memory. The arrangement of bits within a byte can signify different data types, such as integers, floating-point numbers, or characters.

Hexadecimal Notation:

To simplify the representation of binary code, hexadecimal notation is often employed. Hexadecimal (base-16) uses the digits 0-9 and the letters A-F to represent values from 0 to 15. Each hexadecimal digit corresponds to four binary digits (or a nibble), providing a more concise representation. For example, the binary number 11011010 is represented as DA in hexadecimal.

The Significance in Reverse Engineering:

In the realm of reverse engineering, a profound understanding of binary code is paramount. Disassemblers, tools commonly used in reverse engineering, translate machine code—represented in binary—into human-readable assembly language. Analyzing binary code allows reverse engineers to discern the inner workings of software, identify patterns, and unveil the logic encoded by developers.

In conclusion, the mastery of reverse engineering commences with a deep understanding of binary code basics. This foundational knowledge empowers practitioners to navigate the intricate language of computers, providing insights into the core components of software and firmware. As we delve into the subsequent chapters, this comprehension of binary code will serve as the bedrock upon which advanced reverse engineering techniques are built, unlocking the secrets hidden within the digital fabric of technology.

2.2 Techniques for Disassembling Code

Disassembling code is a fundamental skill in reverse engineering, allowing practitioners to analyze the low-level instructions of a compiled program. Disassembly is the process of converting machine code, which is in a binary format, into assembly language or a higher-level programming language that is more human-readable. In this section, we explore various techniques for disassembling code, providing insights into the tools and methodologies used by reverse engineers to unravel the secrets embedded in executable files.

1. Disassemblers:

Disassemblers are specialized tools designed to convert machine code into assembly language. They play a central role in the disassembly process, providing a readable representation of the binary instructions. Popular disassemblers include IDA Pro, Ghidra, OllyDbg, and radare2. These tools offer features such as interactive disassembly, the ability to annotate code, and visualization of control flow graphs, making them essential for reverse engineering tasks.

2. Static Analysis:

Static analysis involves examining the binary code without executing the program. Disassemblers are often used for static analysis, allowing reverse engineers to inspect the code structure, identify functions, and understand the program's logic. During static analysis, disassemblers can provide insights into the relationships between different sections of the code and help in uncovering hidden functionalities.

3. Dynamic Analysis:

Dynamic analysis, in contrast to static analysis, involves running the program and observing its behavior during execution. While disassemblers are commonly associated with static analysis, dynamic analysis tools such as debuggers can also provide disassembly views during runtime. This allows reverse engineers to trace the flow of execution, set breakpoints, and inspect the state of the program as it runs.

4. Function Identification:

One of the primary goals of disassembling code is to identify functions within the program. Functions represent distinct units of code that perform specific tasks. Disassemblers assist in recognizing function boundaries, understanding parameter passing mechanisms, and discerning how functions interact with each other. Function identification is crucial for comprehending the program's overall structure and functionality.

5. Control Flow Analysis:

Disassemblers aid in analyzing the control flow of a program, revealing how the execution moves from one instruction to another. Control flow analysis is essential for understanding the program's logic, identifying decision points (branches), and recognizing loops. Visual representations of control flow graphs provided by disassemblers offer a clear overview of how the program's instructions are interconnected.

6. Annotation and Comments:

Disassemblers allow reverse engineers to annotate code with comments and additional information. This annotation process aids in documenting the understanding of the code, providing insights into the purpose of specific functions or blocks. Comments can include details about variable names, function descriptions, and any other contextual information that enhances the comprehensibility of the disassembled code.

7. Decompilation:

While disassemblers convert machine code to assembly language, decompilers take it a step further by attempting to reconstruct high-level source code. Decompilers analyze the disassembled code and generate a representation that closely resembles the original source code. Although decompiled code might not be identical to the original, it can significantly aid reverse engineers in understanding the program's logic at a higher abstraction level.

8. Pattern Recognition:

Pattern recognition involves identifying recurring sequences of instructions or specific coding patterns within the disassembled code. Recognizing patterns can provide valuable insights into the design choices made by the original developers, help in identifying standard library functions, and facilitate the identification of code structures.

In conclusion, disassembling code is a critical skill for reverse engineers seeking to understand the inner workings of compiled programs. Utilizing disassemblers, combined with static and dynamic analysis techniques, allows practitioners to navigate the complexities of binary code, identify program structures, and uncover the functionalities encoded within executable files. These techniques serve as the bedrock for advanced reverse engineering tasks, enabling practitioners to decipher the intricate language of machine code and gain insights into the logic of software systems.

2.3 Decompilation Fundamentals

Decompilation is a crucial aspect of reverse engineering that takes the process beyond disassembling machine code into the realm of reconstructing a higher-level representation of the original source code. In this section, we delve into decompilation fundamentals, exploring the techniques and challenges involved in translating low-level assembly language back into a more human-readable and comprehensible form.

1. Definition of Decompilation:

Decompilation is the process of converting low-level machine code or assembly language back into a higher-level programming language, attempting to reconstruct the original source code. Unlike disassembly, which provides a one-to-one translation of machine code to assembly language, decompilation aims to recover the algorithmic and structural aspects of the original source code.

2. Intermediate Representation (IR):

During decompilation, an intermediate representation (IR) is often employed as a bridge between assembly language and higher-level source code. The IR is an abstraction that captures the semantics of the original code in a more structured and readable form. It serves as an intermediate step, allowing decompilers to analyze and transform the code into a higher-level language.

3. Challenges in Decompilation:

Decompilation is a challenging task due to several factors, including the loss of information during compilation, optimization techniques applied by compilers, and the inherent ambiguity in translating machine code to a high-level language. Decompilers often encounter situations where multiple high-level constructs could have generated the same machine code, leading to potential ambiguities and challenges in accurate reconstruction.

4. Control Flow Analysis:

Understanding the control flow of the original program is a critical aspect of decompilation. Decompilers analyze the patterns of conditional branches, loops, and function calls to reconstruct the structure of the program. Control flow analysis helps in determining how different parts of the code interact and how the program's logic is organized.

5. Data Flow Analysis:

Data flow analysis is essential for tracking the movement and manipulation of data within the program. Decompilers use data flow analysis to identify variables, their assignments, and how they are used throughout the code. This analysis aids in reconstructing variable names and understanding the relationships between different data elements.

6. Type Inference:

Determining the data types of variables is a crucial aspect of decompilation. Type inference involves analyzing the usage of variables and operations to infer their probable types. While type information may be lost during compilation, decompilers attempt to make educated guesses about the types of variables to improve the accuracy of the reconstructed code.

7. Semantic Analysis:

Decompilers perform semantic analysis to understand the meaning of low-level instructions and translate them into higher-level constructs. This involves recognizing common programming constructs such as conditionals, loops, and function calls and expressing them in a way that aligns with high-level programming languages.

8. Handling Optimization:

Compilers often apply optimization techniques that result in machine code that is more efficient but harder to decompile accurately. Common optimizations include inlining functions, loop unrolling, and dead code elimination. Decompilers must navigate these optimizations to reconstruct the original intent of the code while handling situations where optimization choices may be ambiguous.

9. User Interaction:

Decompilers may provide interactive features, allowing users to assist in the reconstruction process. Users can annotate the code, provide hints to the decompiler, or even manually modify portions of the reconstructed code to improve accuracy. User interaction becomes particularly valuable in cases where the decompiler encounters ambiguity or uncertainty.

10. Output Formats:

Decompilers typically generate output in various formats, including high-level programming languages such as C or C++. The generated code is often accompanied by comments and annotations to convey the level of certainty in the reconstruction. Some decompilers also provide graphical representations of the code's structure, making it easier for reverse engineers to navigate and understand the reconstructed code.

In summary, decompilation is a complex process that involves translating machine code into a higher-level representation, aiming to reconstruct the original source code. By utilizing intermediate representations, control flow analysis, data flow analysis, and semantic analysis, decompilers navigate the challenges posed by the loss of information during compilation and optimization. The user's interaction and the generation of human-readable output contribute to making decompilation an essential tool in the reverse engineer's arsenal for understanding and modifying compiled programs.

2.4 Analyzing Assembly Language Instructions

Analyzing assembly language instructions is a fundamental skill in reverse engineering, providing insight into the low-level operations of a program. Assembly language is a human-readable representation of machine code, and understanding its instructions is crucial for deciphering the functionality and logic encoded in a binary executable. In this section, we explore the basics of analyzing assembly language instructions, covering common instructions, registers, addressing modes, and the role they play in the reverse engineering process.

1. Assembly Language Basics:

Assembly language instructions are symbolic representations of the machine code instructions executed by a computer's central processing unit (CPU). Each instruction corresponds to a specific operation, such as moving data between registers, performing arithmetic operations, or branching based on conditions. Understanding the basics of assembly language involves familiarizing oneself with the mnemonic codes representing these instructions.

2. Registers:

Registers are small, fast storage locations within the CPU that hold data temporarily during program execution. They play a crucial role in assembly language programming, serving as operands for instructions and facilitating data manipulation. Common registers include the program counter (PC), stack pointer (SP), and general-purpose registers (e.g., EAX, EBX, ECX) used for arithmetic and data storage.

3. Addressing Modes:

Addressing modes define how operands are specified in assembly language instructions. Different addressing modes allow for flexibility in accessing data from memory or registers. Common addressing modes include immediate (using a constant value directly), register (operating on data in a register), and indirect (accessing data indirectly through a memory address stored in a register).

4. Arithmetic and Logic Instructions:

Arithmetic and logic instructions perform operations on data, manipulating numerical values or making logical comparisons. Common arithmetic instructions include ADD (addition), SUB (subtraction), and MUL (multiplication). Logic instructions include AND, OR, and XOR, which perform bitwise logical operations on binary values.

5. Control Flow Instructions:

Control flow instructions dictate the flow of execution within a program. Branching instructions, such as JMP (jump), provide a mechanism for changing the program's flow based on conditions. Conditional jumps, like JE (jump if equal) or JG (jump if greater), allow the program to make decisions based on the results of previous operations.

6. Memory Operations:

Memory operations involve moving data between registers and memory locations. Instructions like MOV (move) transfer data, while instructions like LOAD and STORE access values in memory.

Effective analysis of memory operations is essential for understanding how data is manipulated and shared within a program.

7. Stack Operations:

The stack is a region of memory used for storing data in a last-in, first-out (LIFO) fashion. Stack operations include PUSH (pushing data onto the stack) and POP (popping data from the stack). The stack is commonly used for managing function calls, local variables, and maintaining the program's execution context.

8. String and Array Operations:

Some assembly languages provide specialized instructions for working with strings and arrays. For example, REP MOVSB (repeat move byte) is used to efficiently copy blocks of memory, while SCASB (scan byte) is employed for searching within a string.

9. Analyzing Control Flow:

Analyzing control flow in assembly language involves understanding how the program navigates through different sections of code. This includes identifying conditional branches, loops, and subroutine calls. Control flow analysis is crucial for mapping out the program's structure and determining how different parts of the code interact.

10. Debugging and Tracing:

Debuggers, such as OllyDbg or GDB, provide tools for analyzing assembly language instructions during program execution. Debugging allows reverse engineers to step through code, set breakpoints, inspect registers and memory, and gain real-time insights into the program's behavior. Tracing the execution flow aids in understanding how the program evolves over time.

In conclusion, analyzing assembly language instructions is an essential skill in reverse engineering, providing a gateway to understanding the low-level operations of a program. By grasping the basics of assembly language, registers, addressing modes, and common instructions, reverse engineers can decipher the logic encoded in binary executables. This understanding lays the foundation for further exploration into the intricacies of reverse engineering, enabling practitioners to unveil the secrets hidden within the machine code.

3. Reverse Engineering Tools and Environments

Welcome to the toolkit of a reverse engineer—the realm where powerful tools transform complexity into clarity. In this chapter, we embark on an exploration of the diverse ecosystem of reverse engineering tools and environments. We introduce you to the heavyweights like IDA Pro and Ghidra, unveiling their capabilities and guiding you through their functionalities. Setting up your personalized reverse engineering environment becomes a crucial step, and we navigate the landscape to help you assemble the right arsenal for your endeavors. From disassemblers to debuggers, and from hex editors to instrumentation frameworks, each tool plays a unique role in your journey. Join us as we navigate this digital toolbox, empowering you to select the right instruments for the job, transforming the seemingly arcane into the comprehensible, and embarking on a path where mastery of tools is the gateway to mastering reverse engineering.

3.1 Overview of Popular Tools: IDA Pro, Ghidra, etc.

The field of reverse engineering is fortified by a suite of powerful tools that facilitate the analysis of binary executables, disassembly, and decompilation. Among these tools, IDA Pro and Ghidra stand out as stalwarts, each renowned for its unique features and capabilities. In this section, we provide an overview of these popular tools and a few others that play crucial roles in the reverse engineering landscape.

1. IDA Pro:

IDA Pro, developed by Hex-Rays, is one of the most widely used and respected disassemblers in the reverse engineering community. Known for its robust disassembly capabilities, IDA Pro supports a wide range of architectures and file formats. It provides an interactive disassembly interface, graph views of control flow, and a comprehensive plugin system that allows users to extend its functionality. IDA Pro is commonly employed for analyzing and understanding complex binaries, offering both a commercial version and a free version called IDA Free.

2. Ghidra:

Ghidra, developed by the National Security Agency (NSA) and released as open-source software, has gained immense popularity in the reverse engineering community. It offers features comparable to IDA Pro, including disassembly, decompilation, and analysis of binary code. Ghidra supports multiple architectures and file formats, making it versatile for a variety of reverse engineering tasks. Its open-source nature has fostered a collaborative community, contributing to its continual improvement.

3. radare2:

radare2 is an open-source framework for reverse engineering that encompasses a suite of tools for binary analysis, disassembly, and debugging. It provides a command-line interface (CLI) and a graphical user interface (GUI), making it flexible for both experienced users and those new to reverse engineering. radare2 supports a multitude of architectures and file formats, and its modular design allows users to build custom analysis workflows. It is known for its efficiency and extensibility.

4. OllyDbg:

OllyDbg is a popular x86 debugger for Windows, widely used for dynamic analysis and debugging of binary executables. It allows users to step through code, set breakpoints, inspect registers and memory, and analyze the runtime behavior of programs. OllyDbg is especially favored for its ease of use and real-time insights into the execution flow. While its development has slowed, it remains a valuable tool for Windows-centric reverse engineering tasks.

5. x64dbg:

x64dbg is an open-source x86/x64 debugger for Windows that provides a modern and user-friendly interface. It includes features like dynamic analysis, breakpoints, and memory inspection. x64dbg is actively maintained and has a growing community of users. Its plugin system allows for extensibility, enabling users to customize their reverse engineering workflow.

6. Cutter:

Cutter is a graphical interface for radare2, combining the power of radare2 with a user-friendly GUI. It is designed to make radare2 more accessible to users who prefer graphical interfaces. Cutter inherits many features from radare2, including support for various architectures and file formats. The goal is to provide a versatile tool for both beginners and experienced reverse engineers.

7. Binary Ninja:

Binary Ninja is a commercial binary analysis platform known for its modern and user-friendly interface. It provides features such as native code analysis, interactive graph views, and a plugin system for extensibility. Binary Ninja aims to streamline the reverse engineering process by offering an intuitive and efficient environment for analyzing binary code.

8. Hopper Disassembler:

Hopper Disassembler is a commercial disassembler and decompiler for macOS and Linux. It supports various architectures and file formats, offering a range of features for static analysis. Hopper's decompiler assists in translating low-level assembly code into a higher-level representation, making it easier to understand and analyze the functionality of binary executables.

In conclusion, the landscape of reverse engineering tools is diverse, catering to the needs of both beginners and seasoned practitioners. IDA Pro, Ghidra, radare2, and others form an arsenal of tools that empower analysts to dissect, understand, and manipulate binary code. The choice of tool often depends on individual preferences, the specific task at hand, and the target architecture or platform. As the field continues to evolve, these tools play a pivotal role in shaping the practices and methodologies of reverse engineering.

3.2 Setting Up a Reverse Engineering Environment

Setting up a reverse engineering environment involves configuring the necessary tools and resources to effectively analyze and understand binary executables. A well-prepared environment enhances the efficiency and productivity of reverse engineers. Here's a step-by-step guide to setting up a basic reverse engineering environment:

1. Choose an Operating System:

Select an operating system that aligns with your preferences and the requirements of your target binaries. Common choices include Windows, Linux, and macOS. Each operating system has its advantages, and the availability of specific tools may influence your decision.

2. Install Virtualization Software (Optional):

Consider using virtualization software such as VMware, VirtualBox, or Hyper-V to create isolated virtual machines. Virtualization allows you to experiment with potentially malicious binaries in a controlled environment, preserving the integrity of your host system.

3. Set Up a Linux Environment (Optional):

For a Linux-based reverse engineering environment, choose a distribution that suits your needs. Popular choices include Ubuntu, Debian, and Kali Linux. Linux environments are often favored for their extensive toolsets and compatibility with open-source reverse engineering tools.

4. Install Required Tools:

Identify the essential tools for reverse engineering and install them based on your chosen operating system. Some core tools include:

- **IDA Pro or Ghidra**: Install and configure your preferred disassembler and decompiler.
- **radare2**: If you choose to use radare2, install and configure this open-source framework for binary analysis.
- **Debuggers**: Install a debugger such as OllyDbg (Windows), GDB (Linux), or x64dbg (Windows).
- **Cutter**: If using radare2, you may want to install Cutter, a graphical interface for radare2.
- **Binary Ninja or Hopper Disassembler**: Depending on your preference, install a commercial disassembler with advanced features.
- **Python and Scripting Languages**: Many reverse engineering tasks involve scripting. Ensure you have Python or another scripting language installed.

5. Set Up Version Control:

Consider using version control systems such as Git to track changes to your analysis scripts, configurations, and any modifications you make during reverse engineering. This helps maintain a structured and documented approach to your work.

6. Install Additional Tools:

Depending on your specific requirements, install additional tools that complement your reverse engineering tasks. This may include network analysis tools, packet sniffers, or tools for analyzing specific file formats.

7. Create Workspaces:

Organize your reverse engineering projects by creating dedicated workspaces or directories. This helps keep your analysis files, scripts, and documentation well-organized.

8. Stay Updated:

Regularly update your reverse engineering tools to benefit from bug fixes, new features, and security updates. Check for updates to your disassembler, decompiler, debugger, and any other tools you use.

9. Learn Scripting and Automation:

Familiarize yourself with scripting languages like Python or PowerShell. Automation can significantly boost your productivity by allowing you to create custom analysis scripts, automate repetitive tasks, and extract valuable information from binaries.

10. Explore Community Resources:

Join online forums, communities, and platforms dedicated to reverse engineering. Engage with experienced practitioners, seek advice, and stay informed about the latest tools and techniques.

Setting up a reverse engineering environment is a dynamic process that evolves as you gain experience and encounter different challenges. Tailor your environment to suit your specific needs and the nature of the binaries you are analyzing. Regularly explore new tools and techniques to stay at the forefront of the rapidly evolving field of reverse engineering.

3.3 Choosing the Right Tools for Different Tasks

The field of reverse engineering encompasses a diverse set of tasks, ranging from static analysis of binaries to dynamic analysis during runtime. Choosing the right tools for each task is crucial for an effective and efficient reverse engineering workflow. Here, we outline different tasks in reverse engineering and suggest appropriate tools for each:

1. Disassembly:

Tasks: Understanding the low-level instructions of a binary executable, identifying functions, and analyzing control flow.*

Recommended Tools:

- **IDA Pro**: A comprehensive disassembler with advanced features and a user-friendly interface.
- **Ghidra**: An open-source alternative to IDA Pro, offering powerful disassembly and decompilation capabilities.
- **radare2**: A command-line tool for disassembly and binary analysis, known for its flexibility and extensibility.

2. Decompilation:

Tasks: Translating low-level assembly code into a higher-level representation, making it more readable and understandable.*

Recommended Tools:

- **Ghidra**: Known for its robust decompilation capabilities, providing a human-readable view of the original source code.
- **IDA Pro**: Offers a decompiler plugin (Hex-Rays) for generating high-level code from assembly language.
- **Binary Ninja**: Features a decompiler for transforming assembly code into a C-like representation.

3. Debugging:

Tasks: Analyzing binary execution, setting breakpoints, inspecting memory, and understanding runtime behavior.*

Recommended Tools:

- **GDB (GNU Debugger):** A powerful debugger for Linux that supports various architectures.
- **OllyDbg**: A Windows debugger known for its ease of use and real-time analysis capabilities.
- **x64dbg**: An open-source x86/x64 debugger with a modern and user-friendly interface.

4. Dynamic Analysis:

Tasks: Analyzing the behavior of a binary during execution, monitoring system calls, and identifying runtime characteristics.*

Recommended Tools:

- **Process Monitor (ProcMon):** A Windows tool for monitoring file system, registry, and process/thread activity during runtime.
- **Wireshark**: A network protocol analyzer for capturing and analyzing network traffic generated by a binary.
- **Dynamic Instrumentation Tools (e.g., Pin, Frida):** For injecting code dynamically into a running process to analyze its behavior.

5. Scripting and Automation:

Tasks: Creating custom scripts to automate repetitive tasks, extract information, or perform specific analyses.*

Recommended Tools:

- **Python**: A versatile scripting language with extensive libraries, commonly used in the reverse engineering community.
- **PowerShell**: A scripting language for Windows environments, useful for automating tasks and interacting with the system.
- **IDA Python API, GhidraScript**: APIs for scripting within IDA Pro and Ghidra, respectively.

6. Memory Analysis:

Tasks: Analyzing the memory layout of a process, identifying data structures, and understanding memory-related vulnerabilities.*

Recommended Tools:

- **Volatility**: A framework for analyzing memory dumps to extract information about running processes, network connections, and more.

- **WinDbg**: A Windows debugger that can be used for live debugging and post-mortem analysis of memory dumps.
- **GDB with GEF (GDB Enhanced Features):** Enhances GDB with additional features for memory analysis.

7. Binary Patching:

Tasks: Modifying the binary executable to alter its behavior, bypass security measures, or fix vulnerabilities.*

Recommended Tools:

- **Hex Editors (e.g., HxD, 010 Editor):** For manually editing the binary at the hexadecimal level.
- **Patch Management Tools (e.g., BinDiff):** Automated tools for identifying and applying binary patches.

8. Network Analysis:

Tasks: Analyzing network communications initiated by a binary, identifying communication protocols, and monitoring traffic.*

Recommended Tools:

- **Wireshark**: A powerful network protocol analyzer for capturing and analyzing packet-level data.
- **TCPDump**: A command-line packet analyzer for capturing and displaying TCP/IP and other packets on a network.

9. File Format Analysis:

Tasks: Analyzing the structure and contents of specific file formats, such as executables, documents, or image files.*

Recommended Tools:

- **File Format Viewers (e.g., PEView, Hiew):** For examining the structure of binary files.
- **Binwalk**: A tool for analyzing and extracting hidden information in firmware images, documents, and more.

10. Exploitation and Vulnerability Analysis:

Tasks: Identifying and exploiting security vulnerabilities in binaries, understanding potential attack vectors.*

Recommended Tools:

- **Metasploit Framework**: A penetration testing framework that includes tools for identifying and exploiting vulnerabilities.
- **Immunity Debugger**: A powerful debugger with exploit development features for Windows binaries.
- **Pwntools**: A Python library for exploit development and binary exploitation.

Selecting the right tools depends on the specific task at hand, the target platform, and the analyst's familiarity with the toolset. A combination of multiple tools often provides a comprehensive approach to reverse engineering tasks, allowing practitioners to leverage the strengths of each tool in their workflow.

4. Breaking Software Protections

In this chapter, we venture into the realm of digital fortresses and the art of breaching their defenses—Welcome to "Breaking Software Protections." Software protections stand as guardians, and as a reverse engineer, your task is to unravel their secrets. We embark on a journey through the clandestine world of cracking passwords, deciphering encryption schemes, and bypassing license protections. The code becomes your adversary, and we equip you with the techniques to analyze and subvert its resistance. Delve into the intricate dance between protectors and intruders, exploring the strategies employed to secure software and the ingenious methods employed to dismantle those safeguards. As we navigate through this chapter, you'll gain insights into the world of anti-debugging techniques, understanding how to navigate the maze of defenses erected to protect the digital realms. Join us on this expedition, where breaking becomes an art, and software protections are the canvas on which your skills as a reverse engineer unfold.

4.1 Cracking Passwords and Encryption Schemes

Understanding the concepts of password security and encryption is important for individuals pursuing education and careers in cybersecurity and information technology. It's crucial to approach these topics with ethical considerations and legal guidelines in mind. In this educational context, we can explore the principles of password security and encryption, emphasizing responsible and ethical learning.

Password Security:

Password security is a critical aspect of safeguarding digital assets and user accounts. For educational purposes, let's delve into the key principles and considerations without promoting any illicit activities.

Password Strength:

- Passwords should be complex and resistant to brute-force attacks. This involves using a combination of uppercase and lowercase letters, numbers, and special characters.
- Longer passwords are generally more secure. Aim for a minimum of 12 characters.

Password Hashing:

- Storing plaintext passwords is insecure. Systems use cryptographic hashing algorithms to convert passwords into irreversible hashes.
- Common hashing algorithms include SHA-256 and bcrypt. The use of a unique salt for each password enhances security.

Salting:

- Salting involves adding a unique random value (salt) to each password before hashing. This mitigates rainbow table attacks and ensures that identical passwords result in different hashes.

Password Policies:

- Organizations should implement robust password policies that encourage users to create strong passwords and regularly update them.

- Multi-factor authentication (MFA) adds an extra layer of security by requiring additional verification beyond the password.

Educating Users:

- Users play a crucial role in password security. Educational programs should teach users about the importance of strong passwords, avoiding password reuse, and recognizing phishing attempts.

Encryption:

- Encryption is a fundamental technique for securing data, both in transit and at rest. Let's explore encryption principles within ethical and educational contexts.

Symmetric Encryption:

- Symmetric encryption uses a single key for both encryption and decryption. Educational exercises may involve understanding algorithms like AES (Advanced Encryption Standard) and how symmetric keys are shared securely.

Asymmetric Encryption:

- Asymmetric encryption uses a pair of keys: a public key for encryption and a private key for decryption. RSA and ECC (Elliptic Curve Cryptography) are common asymmetric encryption algorithms.
- Understanding how key pairs are generated and used enhances knowledge in this area.

SSL/TLS Protocols:

- SSL (Secure Sockets Layer) and its successor TLS (Transport Layer Security) are cryptographic protocols securing communication over the internet.
- Educational exploration might involve understanding how these protocols establish secure connections and the role of certificates.

End-to-End Encryption:

- End-to-end encryption ensures that data is encrypted on the sender's device and only decrypted on the recipient's device.
- Messaging applications often employ end-to-end encryption to protect user communication.

File and Disk Encryption:

- Tools like BitLocker (Windows), FileVault (macOS), and dm-crypt (Linux) provide disk and file-level encryption.
- Learning about these tools enhances awareness of how encryption safeguards data.

Ethical Considerations:

- While learning about password security and encryption, it's essential to emphasize ethical considerations:

Authorized Learning:

- Only perform activities within environments where you have explicit authorization. Unauthorized attempts to crack passwords or compromise encryption are illegal.

Ethical Hacking:

- Ethical hacking, or penetration testing, involves authorized attempts to identify and rectify security vulnerabilities. This practice adheres to ethical guidelines.

Responsible Use of Knowledge:

- Apply acquired knowledge responsibly. Encourage ethical behavior, respect privacy, and adhere to legal and professional standards.

In conclusion, education in password security and encryption is crucial for individuals entering the field of cybersecurity. Emphasizing ethical considerations ensures that knowledge is applied responsibly and contributes to the improvement of digital security practices. Aspiring professionals should focus on authorized learning, ethical hacking practices, and the responsible use of their knowledge to enhance the overall cybersecurity landscape.

4.2 Analyzing and Defeating Anti-Debugging Techniques

Analyzing and defeating anti-debugging techniques is a topic often explored in ethical hacking, reverse engineering, and cybersecurity research. Understanding how software protects itself from being analyzed or modified is essential for security professionals to identify vulnerabilities, enhance software security, and develop effective defense mechanisms. It's crucial to approach this topic within legal and ethical boundaries, respecting intellectual property rights and adhering to ethical guidelines.

Analyzing Anti-Debugging Techniques:

Anti-debugging techniques are employed by software developers to deter reverse engineering and prevent debugging tools from inspecting the code during runtime. Common anti-debugging techniques include:

Check for Debugger Presence:

Software may perform checks to detect the presence of a debugger, such as examining system flags, checking debugger-related registry keys, or using specific API calls.

Integrity Checks:

Verify the integrity of the running process or specific code sections. If modifications are detected, the software may assume it is being tampered with.

Timing Checks:

Introduce delays or timing checks to detect abnormal pauses, indicating potential debugging attempts. Debuggers may introduce delays in the execution flow, which can be detected by the software.

Exception Handling:

Monitor for exceptions that are commonly triggered during debugging. The presence of certain exceptions may indicate debugging activity.

Code Tracing:

Implement code that intentionally confuses static analysis tools or attempts to detect code tracing and logging.

Defeating Anti-Debugging Techniques:

Security researchers and ethical hackers aim to overcome anti-debugging techniques to analyze and understand the inner workings of software. This is typically done for legitimate purposes, such as identifying vulnerabilities and improving overall system security.

Debugger Detection Bypass:

Modify the binary to bypass checks for the presence of a debugger. This might involve patching conditional jumps or NOP-ing out anti-debugging code.

Dynamic Analysis:

Use dynamic analysis tools that can handle anti-debugging tricks. Dynamic analysis allows researchers to analyze the behavior of the software during runtime, which can be more challenging to protect against.

Memory Modification:

Patch or modify the memory of the running process to bypass integrity checks. This can involve using memory editing tools or techniques.

Timing Manipulation:

Counteract timing checks by modifying the code or using techniques to slow down or accelerate the execution speed.

Exception Handling Bypass:

Use exception handling techniques to suppress or handle exceptions that are commonly triggered during debugging.

Environment Manipulation:

Manipulate the environment in which the software runs, such as modifying registry keys or environment variables, to evade checks that rely on specific configurations.

Ethical Considerations:

It's important to approach the analysis and defeating of anti-debugging techniques ethically and legally:

Authorized Testing:

Conduct such analyses only on systems or software for which you have explicit authorization. Unauthorized attempts to defeat anti-debugging measures may be illegal.

Research and Education:

Engage in such activities for educational or research purposes within ethical boundaries. Understand the legal implications and respect intellectual property rights.

Responsible Disclosure:

If vulnerabilities are discovered, follow responsible disclosure practices. Notify the software vendor or relevant parties to allow for the appropriate patches and updates.

In conclusion, analyzing and defeating anti-debugging techniques is a legitimate aspect of cybersecurity research and ethical hacking. When conducted responsibly, it contributes to improving software security and identifying potential vulnerabilities. Adherence to ethical guidelines and legal considerations is paramount to ensure that these activities are conducted in a lawful and responsible manner.

5. Malware Analysis

Step into the shadows of cyberspace as we delve into the clandestine domain of "Malware Analysis." In this chapter, we equip you with the tools and methodologies to unravel the mysteries hidden within malicious code. Malware, the digital underworld's weapon of choice, conceals its intentions through intricate obfuscation and evasion techniques. We embark on a journey of dynamic and static analysis, peeling back the layers of deception to expose the true nature of these digital adversaries. From dissecting the behavior of malware in a controlled environment to unraveling its secrets without execution, we explore the comprehensive landscape of malware analysis. Unpacking becomes a skill you wield to reveal the core of these digital enigmas, understanding their structure, functionalities, and potential impact. Join us on this expedition, where the shadows hold both danger and discovery, and your expertise as a malware analyst becomes a beacon in the fight against digital threats.

5.1 Introduction to Malware Types

Malware, short for malicious software, is a broad category encompassing various types of harmful software designed to compromise computer systems, steal sensitive information, disrupt normal operations, or gain unauthorized access. Understanding the different types of malware is crucial for cybersecurity professionals, as it allows them to implement effective defenses and countermeasures. In this section, we'll provide an introduction to some common malware types:

1. Viruses:

Viruses are self-replicating programs that attach themselves to other executable files or documents. They often spread through infected email attachments, removable media, or malicious downloads. Once executed, viruses can damage files, corrupt data, or compromise system functionality.

2. Worms:

Worms are standalone programs capable of self-replication and spreading across networks. Unlike viruses, worms do not require a host program to attach to. They exploit vulnerabilities in network protocols or operating systems to propagate rapidly and can cause network congestion or perform malicious actions on infected systems.

3. Trojans (Trojan Horses):

Trojans disguise themselves as legitimate software but carry malicious payloads. Users may unknowingly install Trojans when downloading seemingly harmless applications or files. Once inside a system, Trojans can perform various harmful activities, such as creating backdoors, stealing data, or providing unauthorized access to attackers.

4. Ransomware:

Ransomware encrypts a user's files or entire system, rendering them inaccessible. Attackers then demand a ransom, usually in cryptocurrency, for the decryption key. Ransomware often spreads through phishing emails, malicious attachments, or exploit kits. Recent years have seen a rise in high-profile ransomware attacks targeting individuals, businesses, and even critical infrastructure.

5. Spyware:

Spyware is designed to stealthily collect information about a user's activities without their knowledge. This may include keystrokes, browsing history, login credentials, and other sensitive data. Spyware often infiltrates systems through deceptive downloads or malicious websites.

6. Adware:

Adware displays unwanted advertisements, often in the form of pop-ups or banners, to generate revenue for the attacker. While not inherently malicious, adware can be disruptive and compromise user experience. It typically comes bundled with free software or may be installed unknowingly by users.

7. Botnets:

Botnets consist of a network of compromised computers (bots) controlled by a central command and control (C&C) server. These bots can be used collectively to perform coordinated attacks, such as distributed denial-of-service (DDoS) attacks, spam campaigns, or large-scale data theft.

8. Rootkits:

Rootkits are stealthy malware that conceals its presence by modifying or replacing system-level components. They often target the operating system's kernel, making detection and removal challenging. Rootkits are commonly used to establish persistent access, hide other malware, or maintain control over compromised systems.

9. Keyloggers:

Keyloggers capture and record keystrokes made by a user, including login credentials, credit card numbers, and other sensitive information. These tools may be deployed through malicious websites, email attachments, or other vectors.

10. Fileless Malware:

Fileless malware operates in the system's memory, leaving little to no trace on the disk. These types of malware often leverage legitimate system tools and processes to carry out attacks, making detection more challenging. They may exploit vulnerabilities in software or use social engineering techniques for initial access.

Understanding the characteristics and behaviors of these malware types is essential for developing effective cybersecurity strategies. Security professionals employ a combination of antivirus software, intrusion detection systems, firewalls, and user education to mitigate the risks associated with various malware threats. As the threat landscape evolves, continuous monitoring, threat intelligence, and proactive defense measures become increasingly critical in the ongoing battle against malicious software.

5.2 Dynamic Analysis Techniques

Dynamic analysis is a crucial method in cybersecurity used to examine the behavior of software and malware during runtime. By observing the program's execution in a controlled environment, analysts can uncover its functionalities, interactions, and potential malicious activities. This section introduces various dynamic analysis techniques employed by security professionals to understand and counter malware threats:

1. Sandboxing:

Sandboxing involves executing a program or file in a controlled and isolated environment known as a sandbox. Sandboxes restrict the program's access to the underlying system, allowing analysts to observe its behavior without risking harm to the host system. This technique helps identify malicious activities such as file changes, registry modifications, and network communication.

2. Behavior Analysis:

Behavior analysis focuses on monitoring the actions and interactions of a program during execution. Analysts observe how the software interacts with the operating system, other processes, and network resources. Unusual or malicious behavior, such as unauthorized file access, network communication, or attempts to escalate privileges, can be indicative of malware.

3. Dynamic Code Analysis:

Dynamic code analysis involves examining the actual code execution during runtime. Tools like debuggers and disassemblers allow analysts to step through the code, inspect variables, and identify potential vulnerabilities or malicious functions. This method is particularly useful for understanding how the malware interacts with memory and manipulates code during execution.

4. Memory Analysis:

Memory analysis involves inspecting the content of a program's memory during runtime. Analysts use tools like memory dumpers or forensic frameworks to examine the runtime memory space for signs of malicious activities, injected code, or anomalies. This technique is critical for identifying rootkits, fileless malware, and other memory-resident threats.

5. API Monitoring:

Dynamic analysis often includes monitoring Application Programming Interface (API) calls made by the program. Malware may use specific APIs to interact with the operating system or perform malicious activities. Monitoring these calls helps analysts understand the program's intended functionalities and identify suspicious behavior.

6. Network Traffic Analysis:

Analyzing network traffic generated by a program is essential for understanding its communication patterns. Dynamic analysis tools capture and analyze network traffic to identify potential command-and-control servers, data exfiltration, or communication with malicious entities. This helps in mapping out the infrastructure and intentions of the malware.

7. Dynamic Malware Decryption:

Some malware employs techniques to hide or encrypt their malicious payloads. Dynamic analysis techniques may involve actively analyzing the malware's code execution to identify decryption routines and reveal the hidden malicious content. This allows analysts to uncover the full scope of the threat.

8. Behavioral Profiling:

Behavioral profiling involves creating a profile of normal and expected behavior for a specific system or application. Deviations from this baseline, observed during dynamic analysis, can indicate potentially malicious activities. Behavioral profiling helps in identifying anomalies that may be indicative of a malware infection.

9. Heuristic Analysis:

Heuristic analysis relies on predefined rules and patterns to identify potentially malicious behavior. This approach doesn't rely on known signatures but instead focuses on recognizing behaviors commonly associated with malware. Heuristic analysis tools highlight suspicious activities that may warrant further investigation.

10. Interaction with Emulated Environments:

Emulated environments simulate specific operating systems or system configurations. Dynamic analysis within emulated environments allows analysts to observe how malware behaves under different scenarios. This technique is valuable for understanding the malware's adaptability and evasion techniques.

In conclusion, dynamic analysis techniques play a pivotal role in the cybersecurity landscape, enabling analysts to uncover the behavior of software and identify potential threats. By combining different dynamic analysis methods, security professionals can gain insights into the tactics and techniques employed by malware, allowing for the development of effective countermeasures and improved overall cybersecurity posture.

5.3 Static Analysis Approaches

Static analysis is a cybersecurity technique that involves examining software or malware without executing it. This method is crucial for identifying potential threats, vulnerabilities, and malicious patterns by analyzing the code, file structure, and metadata. Static analysis provides valuable insights into the characteristics of software before it runs. Here are various static analysis approaches employed by security professionals:

1. Code Review:

Code review involves manually examining the source code or disassembled code of a program. Security analysts scrutinize the code for potential vulnerabilities, backdoors, or suspicious functions. This approach is time-intensive but allows for a detailed inspection of the software.

2. Binary Analysis:

Binary analysis involves examining the compiled binary code of a program. Disassemblers and decompilers help convert machine code into human-readable assembly code or higher-level languages. Security professionals analyze the disassembled code to understand the program's logic and potential security issues.

3. Signature-Based Detection:

Signature-based detection relies on known patterns or signatures associated with specific malware or threats. Antivirus software often uses signature databases to identify and block known malicious files. Static analysis helps generate these signatures by extracting unique characteristics from files without running them.

4. Malware Hashing:

Malware hashing involves generating a unique hash value for a file based on its content. Security professionals create hash databases of known malicious files. By comparing the hash of a suspicious file against this database, analysts can quickly identify whether the file is a known threat.

5. Metadata Analysis:

Metadata analysis involves examining metadata associated with files, such as file properties, timestamps, and embedded information. Malicious files may have unusual metadata, and static analysis helps reveal anomalies that can indicate potential threats.

6. String Analysis:

String analysis focuses on extracting and analyzing ASCII or Unicode strings embedded within executable files. Malware often contains unique strings, such as URLs, encryption keys, or command strings. Identifying these strings during static analysis can provide insights into the malware's functionality.

7. Dependency Analysis:

Dependency analysis involves identifying the external libraries, functions, or modules that a program relies on. Security analysts examine these dependencies to understand the potential attack surface and identify any known vulnerabilities associated with the used libraries.

8. Data Flow Analysis:

Data flow analysis traces how data is processed and manipulated within a program. Identifying how user input or external data is handled helps analysts uncover potential security issues, such as input validation vulnerabilities or insecure data handling practices.

9. Control Flow Analysis:

Control flow analysis focuses on understanding the sequence of instructions and paths of execution within a program. Security analysts use this approach to identify potential code vulnerabilities, such as insecure loops, conditional statements, or unintended code execution paths.

10. Automated Static Analysis Tools:

Automated static analysis tools, also known as Static Application Security Testing (SAST) tools, automatically analyze source code or binaries for potential security vulnerabilities. These tools use predefined rules, heuristics, and patterns to identify common security issues.

11. Decompilation:

Decompilation involves reversing the compilation process to convert machine code or bytecode back into a higher-level programming language. Security analysts use decompilers to understand the original source code, identify vulnerabilities, and gain insights into the malware's functionality.

12. YARA Rules:

YARA is a pattern-matching tool that allows analysts to create custom rules for identifying files or code sections based on specific characteristics. Security professionals use YARA rules to detect known or unique patterns associated with malware during static analysis.

In conclusion, static analysis approaches play a crucial role in the early detection and understanding of potential security threats. By examining software without execution, security professionals can identify vulnerabilities, assess the risk level, and implement effective countermeasures to enhance overall cybersecurity.

5.4 Unpacking and Deobfuscation

In the realm of cybersecurity and malware analysis, attackers often employ techniques to obfuscate and pack their malicious code to evade detection by security tools and analysts. Unpacking and deobfuscation are essential processes in the analysis workflow, aimed at revealing the true nature and functionality of a piece of malware. Here's an exploration of these techniques:

1. Obfuscation Techniques:

Code Obfuscation: Malware authors use code obfuscation to make the code more complex and difficult to understand. Techniques may include renaming variables and functions, adding unnecessary code, or using encryption to hide the true behavior of the malware.

String Obfuscation: Malicious strings, such as URLs or command-and-control server addresses, are often obfuscated to make them harder to detect. This involves encoding, encrypting, or splitting strings into parts.

2. Unpacking:

Purpose: Malware authors may use packers or crypters to compress or encrypt their malicious code. Unpacking involves reversing these processes to reveal the original, unpacked code.

Techniques: Analysts use various techniques, such as dynamic analysis in a controlled environment or static analysis of the packed file, to identify and extract the packed payload.

Tools: Unpacking tools and scripts are often developed to automate the unpacking process. These tools attempt to identify and remove the layers of packing applied to the malware.

3. Deobfuscation:

Purpose: Deobfuscation aims to reverse the obfuscation techniques applied to the code, making it more readable and understandable for analysis.

Manual Deobfuscation: Analysts may manually reverse obfuscated code by identifying patterns, understanding the obfuscation techniques used, and reconstructing the original code.

Automated Deobfuscation Tools: Some tools and frameworks automate the deobfuscation process, utilizing algorithms and heuristics to unravel obfuscated code.

4. Techniques for Unpacking and Deobfuscation:

Dynamic Analysis: Running the malware in a controlled environment allows the unpacking process to occur naturally. Observing the behavior of the malware during execution can provide insights into the unpacked code.

Memory Analysis: Analyzing the memory of a process during runtime may reveal the unpacked code. Memory analysis tools can be used to identify and extract the unpacked payload.

Static Analysis: Examining the packed file statically can help identify patterns or signatures associated with common packers. This information aids in selecting appropriate unpacking techniques.

Pattern Recognition: Identifying known packer signatures or obfuscation patterns allows analysts to apply specific techniques or tools tailored to those patterns.

Debugger Usage: Debugging tools, such as OllyDbg or WinDbg, can be employed to step through the code during runtime, helping identify the location of the unpacked payload.

5. Challenges in Unpacking and Deobfuscation:

Anti-Analysis Techniques: Some malware employs anti-analysis techniques to detect when it is being analyzed, making the unpacking process more challenging.

Polymorphic Malware: Polymorphic malware changes its appearance each time it infects a new host, making it difficult to create static signatures for detection.

Self-Modifying Code: Malware that modifies its own code during execution presents challenges for static analysis tools and requires careful handling during dynamic analysis.

6. Manual and Automated Approaches:

Manual Analysis: Skilled analysts use their expertise to manually unpack and deobfuscate malware. This approach is often necessary for sophisticated or custom obfuscation techniques.

Automated Tools: Various automated tools and frameworks assist analysts in the unpacking and deobfuscation process. These tools may be effective for known or less sophisticated obfuscation methods.

7. Importance in Malware Analysis:

Revealing True Intent: Unpacking and deobfuscation are crucial for understanding the true functionality and intent of the malware, enabling analysts to develop effective countermeasures and signatures.

Signature Creation: Unpacked and deobfuscated code provides a basis for creating accurate signatures for detection by antivirus and security software.

In conclusion, unpacking and deobfuscation are integral steps in the malware analysis process. By unraveling the layers of obfuscation applied by malware authors, analysts can gain a clearer understanding of the malicious code, aiding in the development of effective defenses and detection mechanisms. These techniques highlight the ongoing cat-and-mouse game between malware authors and cybersecurity professionals, with each side continuously evolving their tactics.

6. Hardware Reverse Engineering

Welcome to the realm where circuits hum with untold secrets and devices conceal their inner workings—welcome to "Hardware Reverse Engineering." In this chapter, we embark on an exploration of the tangible side of technology, guiding you through the process of dissecting electronic devices and understanding the intricate dance of electrons. From reverse engineering integrated circuits to analyzing PCB layouts, we delve into the hardware landscape with a focus on unlocking the mysteries that lie beneath the surface. The journey takes us through the extraction and examination of firmware from embedded systems, providing a gateway to the code that breathes life into hardware. As a reverse engineer, you become a digital archaeologist, peering into the electronic artifacts of our age to unveil the design choices, vulnerabilities, and hidden functionalities that hardware conceals. Join us in this voyage through the tangible realms of technology, where hardware reverse engineering becomes a bridge between the digital and the physical, and understanding the language of circuits becomes the key to unlocking innovation.

6.1 Reverse Engineering Electronic Devices

Reverse engineering electronic devices involves the systematic analysis and disassembly of a device to understand its components, functionality, and design. This process is commonly used in various industries, including electronics, telecommunications, and cybersecurity, to gain insights into proprietary technology, discover vulnerabilities, or develop compatible solutions. Here, we explore the key aspects and methodologies involved in reverse engineering electronic devices:

1. Device Disassembly:

Purpose: The first step in reverse engineering is physically disassembling the electronic device. This involves opening the device, identifying components, and mapping the internal structure.

Tools: Screwdrivers, prying tools, and other specialized tools are used for non-destructive disassembly. In some cases, destructive methods may be employed, such as de-soldering components for closer examination.

2. Component Identification:

Purpose: Identify and catalog the individual components within the device, including microprocessors, memory chips, sensors, and other integrated circuits.

Methods: Visual inspection, use of magnification tools, and reference to component databases help in identifying and understanding the purpose of each component.

3. Circuit Analysis:

Purpose: Understand the circuitry and connections between components on the device's printed circuit board (PCB).

Tools: Multimeters, oscilloscopes, and other testing equipment are used to trace circuit paths, measure voltages, and analyze signal flows.

4. Reverse Engineering Firmware:

Purpose: Analyze the firmware or software embedded in the device, often stored in microcontrollers or memory chips.

Techniques: Extracting firmware, disassembling code, and analyzing the binary to understand the device's software logic. Tools like disassemblers and decompilers aid in this process.

5. Signal Analysis:

Purpose: Understand how different signals are processed within the device, including communication protocols, data buses, and sensor inputs.

Tools: Oscilloscopes, logic analyzers, and signal generators are used to capture, analyze, and simulate electronic signals.

6. Emulation and Simulation:

Purpose: Emulate or simulate the behavior of the device in a controlled environment to understand its functionality and test modifications.

Tools: Emulation platforms and simulation software help recreate the device's behavior without the need for physical interaction.

7. PCB Reverse Engineering:

Purpose: Create a schematic and layout of the device's PCB to understand the interconnections between components.

Techniques: Visual inspection, circuit tracing, and PCB scanning technologies aid in generating a detailed schematic of the PCB layout.

8. Security Analysis:

Purpose: Identify and analyze security mechanisms, such as encryption, authentication, or secure boot processes, within the device.

Methods: Cryptographic analysis, side-channel attacks, and vulnerability assessments help uncover security weaknesses.

9. Intellectual Property (IP) Extraction:

Purpose: Identify and extract proprietary technologies or intellectual property embedded in the device.

Ethical Considerations: Adhering to legal and ethical standards, as reverse engineering for the purpose of IP theft or infringement is illegal.

10. Documentation and Analysis:

Purpose: Compile detailed documentation of the reverse engineering process, findings, and insights.

Importance: Documenting the process aids in knowledge sharing, future reference, and potential legal compliance.

11. Integration Testing:

Purpose: Validate the understanding gained through reverse engineering by integrating modifications or improvements into the device.

Methods: Testing modified firmware, replacing components, or implementing new features to assess the impact on the device's functionality.

12. Ethical Considerations:

Legal Compliance: Ensure that the reverse engineering process complies with intellectual property laws, end-user license agreements, and ethical standards.

Responsible Disclosure: If vulnerabilities or weaknesses are discovered, follow responsible disclosure practices to notify the device manufacturer and other relevant parties.

In conclusion, reverse engineering electronic devices is a multifaceted process that involves both physical and analytical techniques. Whether undertaken for the purpose of understanding technology, improving compatibility, or identifying security vulnerabilities, it requires a combination of technical skills, ethical considerations, and adherence to legal standards.

6.2 Analyzing Integrated Circuits and PCBs

Analyzing integrated circuits (ICs) and printed circuit boards (PCBs) is a crucial aspect of reverse engineering electronic devices. This process involves dissecting the hardware components to understand their design, functionality, and interactions. Here, we explore the key methodologies and considerations involved in analyzing integrated circuits and PCBs:

1. IC Decapsulation:

Purpose: To expose the internal structure of an integrated circuit, typically by removing the encapsulation material.

Techniques: Chemical etching, acid decapsulation, or mechanical methods may be used. Care must be taken to avoid damaging the IC during this process.

2. Microscopic Analysis:

Purpose: Examine the IC's internal structure and identify individual components and circuitry.

Tools: Microscopes with high magnification capabilities, such as optical microscopes or scanning electron microscopes (SEM), are used for detailed inspection.

3. Die Photography:

Purpose: Capture high-resolution images of the IC's die to aid in further analysis.

Methods: Die shots, obtained through photography or imaging techniques, provide visual insights into the arrangement and structure of transistors and other components on the die.

4. Reverse Engineering ICs:

Purpose: Understand the functionality and design of the integrated circuit.

Techniques: Analyzing the die layout, identifying circuit elements, and reconstructing the schematic are common approaches in reverse engineering ICs. Tools like Electronic Design Automation (EDA) software may be employed.

5. IC Signal Tracing:

Purpose: Trace the paths of signals on the IC to understand how data flows through the circuit.

Tools: Microprobing techniques using fine needles or specialized probes are used to trace signals. This helps in mapping out the internal connections.

6. IC Functional Analysis:

Purpose: Understand the logical functions performed by the integrated circuit.

Methods: By analyzing the circuitry, identifying key components, and observing signal paths, analysts can deduce the functional aspects of the IC.

7. PCB Component Identification:

Purpose: Identify and catalog components on the printed circuit board.

Methods: Visual inspection, magnification tools, and reference to component databases help in identifying resistors, capacitors, ICs, and other components.

8. PCB Layer Analysis:

Purpose: Understand the multilayered structure of the PCB and trace signal paths.

Techniques: X-ray imaging, cross-sectioning, or PCB layer separation methods are used to reveal the internal layers of the board.

9. Signal Integrity Analysis:

Purpose: Assess the integrity of signals as they traverse the PCB.

Tools: Oscilloscopes, signal analyzers, and network analyzers are used to measure signal characteristics, identify noise, and assess signal quality.

10. PCB Reverse Engineering:

Purpose: Create a schematic and layout of the PCB based on analysis.

Techniques: Tracing signal paths, identifying components, and using reverse engineering tools aid in creating an accurate schematic and layout.

11. Embedded System Analysis:

Purpose: Analyze the interaction between the integrated circuits, microcontrollers, and other components in an embedded system.

Techniques: Debugging tools, logic analyzers, and in-circuit emulators help understand the communication and collaboration among different components.

12. Security Analysis:

Purpose: Identify security features, vulnerabilities, and potential attack surfaces within the ICs and PCBs.

Methods: Cryptographic analysis, side-channel attacks, and vulnerability assessments help uncover security weaknesses.

13. Ethical Considerations:

Legal Compliance: Ensure that the analysis complies with intellectual property laws, respecting the manufacturer's rights.

Responsible Use: Reverse engineering should be conducted ethically, and any findings related to security vulnerabilities should follow responsible disclosure practices.

In conclusion, analyzing integrated circuits and PCBs is a meticulous process involving various techniques to understand the inner workings of electronic devices. This knowledge is invaluable for purposes such as product improvement, compatibility enhancement, and uncovering potential security vulnerabilities. Ethical considerations, legal compliance, and responsible practices are essential aspects of conducting effective and ethical reverse engineering in this domain.

6.3 Extracting and Analyzing Firmware from Embedded Systems

Firmware extraction and analysis are critical steps in reverse engineering embedded systems, providing insights into the software that controls the functionality of electronic devices. Whether for understanding proprietary systems, identifying vulnerabilities, or improving compatibility, the process involves uncovering the firmware's structure, logic, and potential security features. Here's an exploration of the methodologies and considerations in extracting and analyzing firmware from embedded systems:

1. Firmware Extraction:

Purpose: Retrieve the firmware stored in embedded systems, typically in microcontrollers or memory devices.

Methods:

Dumping Memory: Extract the contents of the memory or storage device where the firmware is stored.

JTAG Debugging: Utilize Joint Test Action Group (JTAG) interfaces for in-circuit debugging to read and write to memory.

2. Firmware Format Identification:

Purpose: Determine the format of the extracted firmware for further analysis.

Methods:

File Signature Analysis: Identify known file signatures or magic numbers indicative of specific firmware formats.

Header Analysis: Examine the header of the firmware file to understand its structure.

3. File System Extraction:

Purpose: Identify and extract files and data within the firmware, often organized in a file system.

Methods:

File System Analysis Tools: Use tools capable of recognizing and extracting files from common firmware file systems.

Manual Inspection: Analyze the firmware binary for file system structures and extract files manually.

4. Binary Analysis:

Purpose: Understand the logic and functionality of the firmware through binary code analysis.

Methods:

Disassembling: Convert machine code to assembly language to understand the low-level instructions.

Decompilation: Reverse the compilation process to obtain higher-level source code representations.

Symbolic Execution: Simulate the execution of the firmware to understand its behavior.

5. Identifying Functions and Routines:

Purpose: Identify key functions and routines within the firmware to comprehend its functionality.

Methods:

Function Identification: Recognize patterns or behaviors indicative of specific functions.

Symbol Analysis: Leverage symbols or identifiers present in the firmware code to understand the purpose of different code segments.

6. Strings and Constants Analysis:

Purpose: Extract and analyze embedded strings, constants, and textual information within the firmware.

Methods:

String Extraction Tools: Use tools to identify and extract ASCII or Unicode strings from the firmware.

Manual Inspection: Analyze the firmware binary for human-readable strings.

7. Patching and Modification:

Purpose: Modify the firmware for various purposes, such as adding features, bypassing restrictions, or fixing vulnerabilities.

Methods:

Hex Editing: Manually modify the firmware binary using a hex editor.

Patch Management Tools: Use specialized tools designed for firmware patching.

8. Functionality Testing:

Purpose: Validate assumptions and understand the impact of firmware modifications on the embedded system's behavior.

Methods:

Emulation: Emulate the firmware execution in a controlled environment.

In-Circuit Testing: Test the modified firmware on the actual embedded system.

9. Security Analysis:

Purpose: Identify potential security vulnerabilities or weaknesses in the firmware.

Methods:

Static Analysis: Examine the code for common security issues, such as buffer overflows or insecure cryptographic implementations.

Dynamic Analysis: Execute the firmware in a controlled environment to identify runtime vulnerabilities.

10. Cryptographic Analysis:

Purpose: Understand and analyze any cryptographic mechanisms employed in the firmware.

Methods:

Identify Cryptographic Functions: Look for code patterns indicative of encryption or hashing.

Key Extraction: Attempt to extract cryptographic keys used within the firmware.

11. Ethical Considerations:

Legal Compliance: Ensure that the extraction and analysis comply with intellectual property laws and ethical standards.

Responsible Disclosure: If security vulnerabilities are identified, follow responsible disclosure practices to notify relevant parties.

In conclusion, extracting and analyzing firmware from embedded systems is a complex yet essential process in understanding the inner workings of electronic devices. This knowledge can be applied for various purposes, including improving compatibility, uncovering security vulnerabilities, or advancing research and development efforts. Ethical considerations, legal compliance, and responsible disclosure practices are paramount in conducting firmware analysis within ethical boundaries.

7. Network Protocol Reverse Engineering

Step into the complex tapestry of digital communication as we venture into "Network Protocol Reverse Engineering." In this chapter, we unravel the intricacies of the language spoken between devices, exploring the world of communication protocols. From the fundamental principles that govern data exchange to the analysis of network traffic, we equip you with the skills to decipher and manipulate the flow of information. Dive deep into the understanding of protocols used in networked applications, unveiling the underlying structures and patterns. With the ability to dissect and reverse engineer these protocols, you gain the power to navigate the intricate pathways of digital conversations. As we journey through this chapter, you'll explore the art of sniffing and analyzing network traffic, providing you with insights into the inner workings of connected systems. Join us on this expedition, where the language of networks becomes your canvas, and reverse engineering uncovers the hidden narratives in the vast expanse of digital communication.

7.1 Understanding Communication Protocols

Understanding communication protocols is fundamental in the field of reverse engineering, especially when analyzing how different electronic devices or software systems communicate with each other. Communication protocols define the rules and conventions for exchanging information, and reverse engineering these protocols is crucial for interoperability, security analysis, and gaining insights into the inner workings of a system. Here's an exploration of the key aspects involved in understanding communication protocols:

1. Definition of Communication Protocols:

Purpose: Establish a common set of rules and conventions for devices or systems to exchange data.

Elements:

- **Message Format**: Specification of how data is structured in a message.
- **Message Encoding**: Rules for representing data in a binary or textual format.
- **Message Timing**: Timing and synchronization rules for message transmission.
- **Error Handling**: Procedures for detecting and handling errors in communication.

2. Types of Communication Protocols:

- **Serial Protocols**: Data is transmitted sequentially, bit by bit, over a single wire or a pair of wires. Examples include UART, SPI, and I2C.
- **Parallel Protocols**: Multiple bits are transmitted simultaneously over separate wires. Examples include PCI, IDE, and parallel printer interfaces.
- **Network Protocols**: Govern data exchange in computer networks. Examples include TCP/IP, HTTP, and UDP.
- **Wireless Protocols**: Govern communication in wireless networks. Examples include Wi-Fi, Bluetooth, and Zigbee.
- **Industrial Protocols**: Used in industrial automation and control systems. Examples include Modbus, Profibus, and CAN.

3. Protocol Analysis Tools:

- **Packet Sniffers**: Tools that capture and analyze data packets exchanged between devices on a network.
- **Logic Analyzers**: Hardware devices that capture and display digital signals for analyzing communication between components.
- **Protocol Analyzers**: Specialized tools designed for decoding and analyzing specific communication protocols.

4. Protocol Reverse Engineering Process:

- **Packet Capture**: Capture sample communication packets or messages between devices.
- **Traffic Analysis**: Analyze the captured traffic to identify patterns, headers, and data fields.
- **Message Decoding**: Decode the captured messages to understand the structure and meaning of different fields.
- **State Machine Analysis**: Identify the state transitions and behaviors of devices based on communication patterns.
- **Message Injection**: Modify and inject messages to observe how the system responds.

5. Message Format and Structure:

- **Header**: Contains information about the message, such as its type, source, destination, and length.
- **Data Payload**: Carries the actual data being transmitted.
- **Checksum or CRC**: Provides a mechanism for error detection.
- **Footer**: Marks the end of the message.

6. Analyzing Network Protocols:

- **TCP/IP Suite**: Understand the layers of the TCP/IP protocol stack, including the roles of protocols like IP, TCP, UDP, and ICMP.

- **HTTP/HTTPS Analysis**: Analyze web communication, including request and response formats.
- **DNS Analysis**: Understand how domain name resolution works and analyze DNS messages.
- **Wireless Network Protocols**: Analyze protocols specific to wireless communication, such as Wi-Fi or Bluetooth.

7. Industrial Protocol Analysis:

- **Modbus Analysis**: Understand the Modbus protocol used in industrial automation.
- **CAN Bus Analysis**: Analyze the communication on Controller Area Network (CAN) buses used in automotive and industrial applications.
- **Profibus Analysis**: Explore the Profibus protocol commonly used in manufacturing and process automation.

8. Security Implications:

- **Vulnerability Identification**: Protocol analysis can help identify vulnerabilities in the communication process.
- **Man-in-the-Middle Attacks**: Understanding protocols aids in identifying and mitigating man-in-the-middle attacks.
- **Encryption Analysis**: Analyze how encryption is implemented within the communication protocol.

9. Ethical Considerations:

- **Legal Compliance**: Ensure that the reverse engineering of communication protocols complies with relevant laws and regulations.
- **Responsible Use**: Use the knowledge gained from protocol analysis responsibly, avoiding any actions that could lead to unauthorized access or harm.

In conclusion, understanding communication protocols is a foundational skill in reverse engineering, enabling analysts to decipher the language spoken between devices. This knowledge is vital for achieving interoperability, ensuring security, and gaining a deeper understanding of the systems being analyzed. Ethical considerations and responsible use are essential aspects of applying protocol reverse engineering in a lawful and ethical manner.

7.2 Sniffing and Analyzing Network Traffic

Network traffic analysis plays a crucial role in reverse engineering, providing insights into the communication patterns and data exchanges between devices in a network. Sniffing network traffic involves capturing and analyzing the data packets flowing between devices, helping reverse engineers understand protocols, identify vulnerabilities, and gain a comprehensive view of system interactions. Here's an exploration of the key aspects involved in sniffing and analyzing network traffic:

1. Packet Sniffing Overview:

Purpose: Capture and inspect data packets flowing through a network.

Tools:

- **Wireshark**: A widely used, open-source packet analyzer.
- **Tcpdump**: A command-line packet analyzer for Unix-like systems.
- **Fiddler**: A web debugging proxy that captures HTTP traffic.
- **Ethereal**: Former name for Wireshark.

2. Network Topology Considerations:

- **Hub-Based Networks**: In hub-based networks, all traffic is broadcasted to every connected device, making it easy to capture packets.
- **Switched Networks**: In switched networks, a switch directs traffic only to the intended recipient. Techniques like ARP poisoning may be used to redirect traffic to the sniffing device.

3. Types of Network Traffic:

- **Unicast**: One-to-one communication between a sender and a specific recipient.
- **Multicast**: One-to-many communication, where data is sent to a group of devices.
- **Broadcast**: One-to-all communication, where data is sent to all devices in the network.

4. Sniffing Techniques:

- **Promiscuous Mode**: Network interfaces operating in promiscuous mode can capture all packets on the network, even those not destined for the capturing device.
- **ARP Spoofing/Poisoning**: Redirects traffic through the sniffing device by manipulating ARP (Address Resolution Protocol) tables.
- **MAC Flooding**: Overloads the switch's MAC address table, causing it to operate like a hub and broadcasting all traffic to all devices.

5. Wireshark Basics:

- **Capture Filters**: Specify criteria for capturing specific types of traffic.
- **Display Filters**: Filter and analyze captured packets based on various criteria.

- **Packet Details**: View detailed information about each packet, including source and destination addresses, protocols, and payload.

6. Protocol Analysis:

- **Common Protocols**: Analyze traffic to identify common protocols like TCP, UDP, ICMP, HTTP, DNS, etc.
- **Header Inspection**: Examine the headers of packets to understand the structure of different protocols.
- **Flow Analysis**: Identify communication flows and sequences between devices.

7. Identifying Anomalies:

- **Unusual Traffic Patterns**: Detect unusual patterns, such as high data volume or unexpected communication between devices.
- **Abnormal Protocols**: Identify the use of non-standard or unexpected protocols.
- **Unexpected Devices**: Discover devices on the network that were not previously known.

8. Reconnaissance and Enumeration:

- **Discovering Devices**: Use sniffed traffic to identify devices on the network.
- **Enumerating Services**: Analyze protocols to understand the services and applications running on devices.

9. Vulnerability Identification:

- **Unencrypted Passwords**: Detect the transmission of unencrypted passwords or sensitive information.
- **Security Protocol Analysis**: Identify weaknesses in security protocols or encryption implementations.

- **Injection Attacks**: Look for signs of injection attacks, such as SQL injection or command injection.

10. Malware and Intrusion Detection:

- **Behavioral Analysis**: Observe network behavior to detect patterns indicative of malware or intrusion attempts.
- **Signature-based Detection**: Use known patterns or signatures to identify malicious activities in the network traffic.

11. Ethical Considerations:

- **Legal Compliance**: Ensure that network sniffing activities comply with applicable laws and regulations.
- **Privacy**: Respect privacy considerations, avoiding the interception of sensitive or personal information.
- **Responsible Use**: Use network sniffing for legitimate purposes, such as network troubleshooting, security assessments, or research.

In conclusion, sniffing and analyzing network traffic are essential skills in reverse engineering, providing a wealth of information about system interactions and communication protocols. Ethical considerations, legal compliance, and responsible use are crucial aspects of employing network sniffing techniques in a lawful and ethical manner.

7.3 Reverse Engineering Networked Applications and Protocols

Reverse engineering networked applications and protocols involves dissecting the communication between software systems over a network. This process is essential for understanding how applications interact, identifying protocol structures, and uncovering the logic behind networked functionalities. Here's an exploration of the key aspects involved in reverse engineering networked applications and protocols:

1. Application Layer Analysis:

- **Packet Structure**: Analyze the structure of packets exchanged between applications.
- **Message Types**: Identify different types of messages or requests exchanged at the application layer.
- **Message Format**: Understand the format of data within application layer messages.

2. Protocol Identification:

- **Port Scanning**: Identify open ports on networked systems to understand which applications are running.
- **Service Fingerprinting**: Analyze responses from networked services to determine the protocols and applications in use.

3. Capture and Inspection:

- **Packet Capture**: Use tools like Wireshark to capture network traffic between applications.
- **Data Payload Analysis**: Inspect the payload of packets to understand the actual data being transmitted.
- **Request-Response Analysis**: Identify patterns in the communication flow, including request-response pairs.

4. Session Analysis:

- **Session Establishment**: Understand the process of establishing a session or connection between applications.
- **Session Maintenance**: Analyze how sessions are maintained and managed during ongoing communication.

- **Session Termination**: Investigate how sessions are terminated or closed between applications.

5. Message Encryption and Compression:

- **Encryption Analysis**: Identify encrypted portions within messages and analyze encryption algorithms if applicable.
- **Compression Detection**: Detect the use of compression algorithms in transmitted data.

6. Authentication Mechanisms:

- **User Authentication**: Analyze how user authentication is handled within networked applications.
- **Token-Based Authentication**: Investigate the use of tokens or session keys for authentication purposes.
- **Authorization Process**: Understand how authorization and access control are implemented.

7. State Management:

- **Session State**: Analyze how session state is managed between client and server.
- **Cookies and Tokens**: Examine the use of cookies or tokens for maintaining state information.

8. API Endpoints and End-User Actions:

- **Identifying API Endpoints**: Discover the various API endpoints used by networked applications.
- **Mapping User Actions**: Understand how end-user actions translate into requests and responses at the network level.

9. Web Application Analysis:

- **HTTP(S) Traffic Analysis**: Analyze HTTP(S) traffic to understand web application interactions.
- **WebSockets Analysis**: Investigate the use of WebSockets for real-time communication in web applications.
- **AJAX Requests**: Understand how Asynchronous JavaScript and XML (AJAX) requests contribute to dynamic web application behavior.

10. Binary Protocol Analysis:

- **Binary Packet Structure**: Analyze the structure of binary packets used in custom protocols.
- **Serialization Formats**: Identify the serialization formats used for encoding data in binary protocols.

11. Malicious Traffic Detection:

- **Anomaly Detection**: Employ anomaly detection techniques to identify unusual or malicious network behavior.
- **Signature-Based Detection**: Use known patterns or signatures to identify specific types of malicious activity.

12. Vulnerability Identification:

- **Input Validation**: Examine how input validation is implemented to identify potential injection vulnerabilities.
- **Buffer Overflows**: Analyze networked applications for potential buffer overflow vulnerabilities.
- **Security Misconfigurations**: Identify misconfigurations in networked applications that may lead to security issues.

13. Simulating Interactions:

- **Replay Attacks**: Simulate the replay of captured network interactions to understand the impact on the application.

- **Input Manipulation**: Modify input parameters during network interactions to observe application responses.

14. Ethical Considerations:

- **Legal Compliance**: Ensure that reverse engineering activities comply with relevant laws and regulations.
- **Responsible Disclosure**: If vulnerabilities are identified, follow responsible disclosure practices to notify relevant parties.
- **Privacy Considerations**: Respect privacy concerns and avoid intercepting sensitive or personal information.

In conclusion, reverse engineering networked applications and protocols is a multifaceted process that requires a deep understanding of communication flows, application behaviors, and underlying protocols. Ethical considerations, including legal compliance and responsible disclosure, are paramount to ensure that these activities are conducted in an ethical and lawful manner.

8. Mobile Application Reverse Engineering

Enter the dynamic world of pocket-sized technologies as we embark on the exploration of "Mobile Application Reverse Engineering." In this chapter, we unveil the secrets held within the apps that define our daily interactions with smartphones and tablets. From dissecting Android and iOS applications to peering into the intricacies of mobile code, we guide you through the process of unraveling the functionalities and security measures embedded in mobile applications. Decompilation becomes your tool of choice, enabling you to traverse the layers of abstraction and understand the logic behind the mobile user interface. With an emphasis on modifying and patching mobile applications, we empower you to explore the boundaries of customization and innovation within the mobile landscape. Join us in this chapter as we navigate the evolving terrain of mobile technology, where reverse engineering becomes the gateway to understanding and manipulating the software that shapes our digital experiences.

8.1 Analyzing Android and iOS Apps

Analyzing mobile applications for Android and iOS involves dissecting the binaries, understanding the application's behavior, and uncovering potential security vulnerabilities. This process is crucial for app developers, security professionals, and researchers aiming to enhance app security, identify weaknesses, and gain insights into the app's inner workings. Here's an exploration of the key aspects involved in analyzing Android and iOS apps:

1. App Binary Analysis:

- **Decompilation**: Convert the compiled binary code (APK for Android, IPA for iOS) into human-readable code for analysis.
- **Tools**: Use tools like JADX for Android or Hopper Disassembler for iOS to decompile binaries.

2. Understanding App Architecture:

- **Components Analysis**: Identify and understand the different components of the app, such as activities, services, and broadcast receivers.
- **App Lifecycle**: Understand the lifecycle events and transitions within the app.

3. Reverse Engineering Resources:

- **Layouts and UI Elements**: Analyze XML layouts (Android) or nib files (iOS) to understand the app's user interface.
- **Asset Analysis**: Inspect embedded assets, such as images or multimedia files, to gain insights into the app's resources.

4. Inter-Component Communication:

- **Intent Analysis (Android):** Examine how different components communicate using intents in Android.
- **URL Scheme Analysis (iOS):** Investigate how different components interact using URL schemes in iOS.

5. API and Network Communication:

- **API Endpoint Discovery**: Identify the backend APIs the app communicates with.
- **Traffic Analysis**: Capture and analyze network traffic to understand data exchanged between the app and servers.
- **TLS/SSL Inspection**: Decrypt and inspect encrypted traffic for security analysis.

6. Security Token Handling:

- **Token Analysis**: Identify how security tokens, such as session tokens or API keys, are generated, stored, and transmitted.
- **OAuth and OpenID Connect (OIDC):** Analyze how OAuth and OIDC protocols are implemented for user authentication.

7. Dynamic Analysis:

- **Runtime Behavior**: Use dynamic analysis tools to observe the app's behavior during runtime.
- **Instrumentation**: Inject instrumentation code to monitor specific functions or events within the app.

8. Code Injection and Hooking:

- **Method Hooking (Android/iOS):** Inject code into app processes to intercept and modify method calls.
- **Jailbreak/Root Detection Bypass**: Analyze how the app detects jailbroken (iOS) or rooted (Android) devices and bypass these checks if necessary.

9. Vulnerability Identification:

- **Secure Storage Analysis**: Check how sensitive data, such as passwords or tokens, is stored and encrypted.
- **Input Validation**: Identify potential injection points and test input validation mechanisms.
- **Webview Security**: Analyze the security of webviews, ensuring they are not susceptible to common web vulnerabilities.

10. Static Analysis Tools:

- **Linting (Android):** Use Android Lint to identify issues related to performance, security, and correctness.
- **Static Analyzer (iOS):** Leverage static analysis tools like Clang Static Analyzer to find potential issues in iOS code.

11. App Obfuscation and Anti-Reversing Techniques:

- **Code Obfuscation**: Analyze how code obfuscation is implemented to deter reverse engineering.
- **Anti-Tampering Measures**: Identify mechanisms that prevent or detect tampering with the app binary.

12. Third-Party Library Analysis:

- **Library Identification**: Identify and analyze third-party libraries used in the app.
- **Security of Third-Party Components**: Assess the security posture of integrated libraries for potential vulnerabilities.

13. Privacy Considerations:

- **Data Handling**: Assess how user data is handled and stored, ensuring compliance with privacy regulations.
- **Permissions Analysis**: Review the permissions requested by the app and ensure they are necessary for its functionality.

14. Ethical Considerations:

- **Legal Compliance**: Ensure that the analysis of mobile apps complies with relevant laws and terms of service.
- **Responsible Disclosure**: If security vulnerabilities are identified, follow responsible disclosure practices to notify app developers.

In conclusion, analyzing Android and iOS apps involves a combination of static and dynamic analysis techniques to understand the app's structure, behavior, and potential security risks. Ethical considerations, including legal compliance and responsible disclosure, are essential to ensure that app analysis is conducted ethically and within the bounds of applicable regulations.

8.2 Decompiling Mobile Code

Decompiling mobile code is a critical process in reverse engineering, enabling the examination of the underlying source code of mobile applications. This is essential for understanding an app's functionality, identifying vulnerabilities, and uncovering potential security risks. Here's an exploration of the key aspects involved in decompiling mobile code for both Android (APK) and iOS (IPA) applications:

1. Android App Decompilation (APK):

- **Tool Usage**: Utilize tools such as JADX, jadx-gui, or JADX-DEX2JAR to decompile Android APK files.
- **Java Source Code**: Analyze the decompiled code to view the Java source code of the application.
- **Resource Extraction**: Extract and examine resources, including layouts, images, and other assets.

2. iOS App Decompilation (IPA):

- **Tool Usage**: Tools like Hopper Disassembler, IDA Pro, or Ghidra can be used for disassembling iOS applications.
- **Objective-C/Swift Code**: Review the disassembled code to understand the Objective-C or Swift source code of the application.

- **Nib File Inspection**: Explore NIB/XIB files to understand the app's user interface components.

3. Decompiled Code Analysis:

- **Functionality Identification**: Analyze the decompiled code to identify key functionalities and components.
- **Method Calls**: Examine method calls to understand how different parts of the application interact.
- **Library and API Usage**: Identify third-party libraries and APIs used by the application.

4. Reconstructing High-Level Code:

- **Manual Reconstruction**: Enhance readability by manually improving the structure and organization of the decompiled code.
- **Variable and Function Naming**: Rename variables and functions to provide meaningful names for easier comprehension.

5. Handling Obfuscated Code:

- **Obfuscation Techniques**: Understand common obfuscation techniques used to hinder decompilation.
- **Deobfuscation Strategies**: Employ deobfuscation techniques to make the code more understandable.

6. Identifying Entry Points:

- **Main Entry Point**: Identify the main entry point or starting function of the application.
- **Event Handlers**: Locate functions associated with user interface events or external triggers.

7. Resource and Asset Analysis:

- **Layout Files (Android):** Analyze XML layout files to understand the app's user interface structure.
- **Nib Files (iOS):** Explore NIB/XIB files to inspect the layout and structure of iOS app interfaces.
- **Images and Resources**: Examine embedded images and resources to gain insights into the app's visual elements.

8. API Endpoint Discovery:

- **Network-Related Code**: Investigate code related to network communications to identify API endpoints.
- **HTTP Requests (iOS/Android):** Examine code making HTTP requests to understand data exchanges with servers.

9. Security Token Handling:

- **Token Extraction**: Identify how security tokens are generated, stored, and transmitted within the decompiled code.
- **OAuth and OIDC Implementation**: Analyze the implementation of OAuth and OpenID Connect protocols for user authentication.

10. Static Analysis Tools:

- **Code Linters**: Utilize code linters to identify potential issues related to security, performance, and code correctness.
- **Security Scanners**: Use static analysis tools to scan for security vulnerabilities in the decompiled code.

11. Patching and Modification:

- **Code Modification**: Experiment with code modifications to understand the impact on app behavior.

- **Patch Testing**: Test patches on the decompiled code to observe changes in functionality.

12. Ethical Considerations:

- **Legal Compliance**: Ensure that decompilation activities adhere to relevant laws and terms of service.
- **Responsible Use**: Use the knowledge gained from decompilation ethically and responsibly, avoiding misuse or unauthorized actions.

In conclusion, decompiling mobile code is a powerful technique in reverse engineering, providing valuable insights into the inner workings of Android and iOS applications. Ethical considerations, legal compliance, and responsible use are crucial to ensure that decompilation is conducted ethically and within the bounds of applicable regulations.

8.3 Modifying and Patching Mobile Applications

Modifying and patching mobile applications involves altering the code, resources, or behavior of an application for various purposes, such as customization, security testing, or research. While this process can provide valuable insights, it's important to approach it ethically and in compliance with relevant laws. Here's an exploration of the key aspects involved in modifying and patching mobile applications for both Android and iOS:

1. Decompilation and Code Modification:

- **Decompilation Process**: Use tools like JADX (Android) or Hopper Disassembler (iOS) to decompile the mobile app's binary code.

- **Code Modification**: Identify specific areas in the decompiled code that need modification for the desired outcome.

2. Resource Modification:

- **Layout and UI Changes (Android):** Modify XML layout files to alter the user interface structure.
- **Asset Replacement**: Replace or modify embedded images and resources to customize the app's appearance.

3. Method Hooking and Injection:

- **Method Hooking (Android/iOS):** Inject custom code to intercept and modify the behavior of specific methods.
- **Dynamic Link Library (DLL) Injection (iOS):** Inject custom dynamic libraries into the app's process space to modify behavior.

4. Patching Security Vulnerabilities:

- **Identifying Vulnerabilities**: Analyze the decompiled code for security vulnerabilities, such as input validation issues or insecure storage.
- **Code Modification for Fixes**: Patch the code to fix identified vulnerabilities and enhance security.

5. Customization and Theming:

- **User Interface Customization**: Modify UI elements and layouts to create custom themes.
- **Color and Style Changes**: Adjust color schemes and styles to customize the visual appearance of the app.

6. Feature Unlocking and Bypassing Restrictions:

- **Removing Ads:** Disable or remove advertisements by modifying relevant code.
- **Unlocking Premium Features**: Bypass restrictions to access premium features without a subscription.

7. Jailbreak/Root Detection Bypass:

- **Identifying Detection Mechanisms**: Analyze code related to jailbreak (iOS) or root (Android) detection.
- **Code Modification**: Patch the code to bypass jailbreak/root detection mechanisms.

8. In-App Purchase Bypass:

- **Identifying Purchase Checks**: Analyze code responsible for checking in-app purchases.
- **Bypassing Purchase Checks**: Modify the code to bypass purchase checks and unlock in-app content.

9. Testing Patches:

- **Emulator and Simulator Testing**: Test modified apps in emulators (Android) or simulators (iOS) to observe changes.
- **Real Device Testing**: Deploy patched apps to real devices to assess behavior in a more realistic environment.

10. Dynamic Analysis of Modified Apps:

- **Runtime Behavior Observation**: Use dynamic analysis tools to observe how the modified app behaves during runtime.
- **Instrumentation for Monitoring**: Inject instrumentation code to monitor specific functions or events in the patched app.

11. Legal and Ethical Considerations:

- **Terms of Service Compliance**: Ensure that modifying or patching apps complies with the app's terms of service.
- **Intellectual Property Rights**: Respect the intellectual property rights of app developers.
- **Responsible Use**: Avoid unauthorized or malicious use of modified apps and share findings responsibly.

12. Reversibility and Backups:

- **Backup Original Apps**: Before making modifications, create backups of the original app binaries.
- **Reversibility**: Ensure that modifications can be reversed, and the app can be restored to its original state.

13. Ethical Hacking and Security Research:

- **Security Testing**: Use modified apps for ethical hacking and security research to identify vulnerabilities.
- **Reporting Vulnerabilities**: If security issues are identified, follow responsible disclosure practices to report findings to app developers.

In conclusion, modifying and patching mobile applications can be a valuable tool for customization, testing, and research. Ethical considerations, legal compliance, and responsible use are paramount to ensure that these activities are conducted ethically and within the bounds of applicable laws and terms of service.

9. Web Application Reverse Engineering

Step into the virtual realm of interconnected websites and dynamic interfaces as we explore "Web Application Reverse Engineering." In this chapter, we unravel the intricacies of web-based technologies, guiding you through the process of dissecting and understanding the components that drive the online world. From inspecting and manipulating web traffic to analyzing JavaScript and front-end code, we delve into the layers that constitute modern web applications. Reverse engineering APIs and server-side logic becomes your expertise, allowing you to uncover the inner workings of cloud-based systems. As we navigate through this chapter, you'll gain insights into the strategies employed to decode the language of the web, offering you the ability to analyze, modify, and innovate within the digital frontier. Join us in this exploration where web application reverse engineering becomes a key to unlocking the secrets of the online landscape and understanding the code that powers our interconnected experiences.

9.1 Inspecting and Manipulating Web Traffic

Inspecting and manipulating web traffic is a fundamental skill in the field of reverse engineering, allowing analysts to understand the communication between clients and servers, identify vulnerabilities, and manipulate data for various purposes. Here's an exploration of the key aspects involved in inspecting and manipulating web traffic:

1. Proxy Setup:

- **Use of Proxy Servers**: Employ proxy servers like Burp Suite, Charles Proxy, or Fiddler to intercept and inspect web traffic.
- **Configuring Web Browsers**: Set up web browsers to route traffic through the proxy for analysis.

2. Intercepting HTTP(S) Traffic:

- **HTTP Traffic Analysis**: Capture and inspect HTTP requests and responses exchanged between clients and servers.
- **HTTPS Traffic Decryption**: Implement SSL/TLS interception to decrypt and analyze encrypted HTTPS traffic.

3. Request and Response Inspection:

- **Header Analysis**: Examine HTTP headers to understand details such as user-agent, content type, and cookies.
- **Body Content Inspection**: Inspect the content of request and response bodies for data parameters and payloads.

4. Modifying Requests:

- **Parameter Manipulation**: Modify request parameters to observe the impact on server responses.
- **Cookie Modification**: Edit cookies to test session-related vulnerabilities or customize user-specific data.

5. Response Manipulation:

- **Content Injection**: Inject content into server responses to test for vulnerabilities like Cross-Site Scripting (XSS).
- **Filtering Content**: Modify or filter specific content in responses for testing or analysis.

6. Session Management:

- **Session Token Analysis**: Analyze how session tokens are generated, transmitted, and validated.
- **Session Hijacking Tests**: Manipulate session-related data to test for session hijacking vulnerabilities.

7. Authentication Testing:

- **Login Form Analysis**: Inspect the authentication process, including parameters sent during login attempts.
- **Brute Force Testing**: Test authentication mechanisms for susceptibility to brute force attacks.

8. Cross-Origin Resource Sharing (CORS) Testing:

- **CORS Header Analysis**: Analyze CORS headers to understand and test cross-origin restrictions.
- **Origin Manipulation**: Test for potential security issues related to cross-origin requests.

9. WebSockets and Real-Time Communication:

- **WebSocket Inspection**: Capture and analyze WebSocket communication for real-time applications.
- **Event Triggering**: Manipulate WebSocket messages to test how the application responds.

10. Security Headers Analysis:

- **HTTP Security Headers**: Inspect the presence and configuration of security headers like Content Security Policy (CSP) and Strict-Transport-Security (HSTS).
- **Header Injection Testing**: Test for security issues related to HTTP header injection.

11. API Endpoint Discovery:

- **URL and Parameter Analysis**: Identify API endpoints by analyzing URLs and request parameters.
- **REST API Testing**: Inspect and test the functionality of RESTful APIs.

12. Load and Performance Testing:

- **Request Timing Analysis**: Measure and analyze the timing of requests for performance testing.
- **Concurrency Testing**: Test the application's behavior under concurrent or high-load conditions.

13. Dynamic Analysis Tools:

- **Burp Suite Tools**: Utilize Burp Suite's features like Intruder, Repeater, and Sequencer for dynamic analysis.
- **Charles Proxy Tools**: Leverage tools within Charles Proxy for dynamic traffic manipulation and inspection.

14. Mobile App Traffic Inspection:

- **Proxying Mobile App Traffic**: Intercept and inspect web traffic generated by mobile applications using proxy tools.
- **Emulator/Simulator Testing**: Analyze how mobile apps communicate with servers during runtime.

15. Legal and Ethical Considerations:

- **Data Privacy Compliance**: Ensure that web traffic inspection activities comply with data privacy regulations.
- **Responsible Use:** Use the knowledge gained from traffic inspection ethically and responsibly, avoiding unauthorized access or misuse.

In conclusion, inspecting and manipulating web traffic is a powerful technique for understanding, testing, and securing web applications. Adhering to legal and ethical considerations is essential to ensure that these activities are conducted in a responsible and lawful manner.

9.2 Analyzing JavaScript and Front-end Code

Analyzing JavaScript and front-end code is crucial for understanding the behavior of web applications, identifying security vulnerabilities, and reverse engineering complex client-side logic. Here's an exploration of the key aspects involved in analyzing JavaScript and front-end code:

1. Source Code Inspection:

- **Browser Developer Tools**: Utilize browser developer tools (Chrome DevTools, Firefox Developer Tools) to inspect and debug JavaScript code.
- **Viewing Source Code**: Explore the original source code by inspecting files loaded in the browser.

2. JavaScript Debugging:

- **Setting Breakpoints**: Place breakpoints in the code to pause execution and inspect variables and states.
- **Stepping Through Code**: Use debugging tools to step through JavaScript code line by line for in-depth analysis.

3. Static Analysis:

- **Code Linters**: Employ code linters (ESLint, JSHint) to identify syntax errors, coding style issues, and potential vulnerabilities.
- **Code Complexity Analysis**: Use tools to assess code complexity and identify areas that may require refactoring.

4. Dynamic Analysis:

- **Runtime Behavior Observation**: Observe the behavior of JavaScript code during runtime using debugging tools.
- **Dynamic Instrumentation**: Inject instrumentation code to monitor specific functions or events in the front-end code.

5. Identifying Third-Party Libraries:

- **Library Recognition**: Identify and analyze third-party libraries used in the application.
- **Security Assessment**: Assess the security of integrated libraries for potential vulnerabilities.

6. DOM Manipulation Analysis:

- **DOM Inspection**: Inspect the Document Object Model (DOM) structure to understand how JavaScript manipulates the DOM.
- **Event Binding**: Identify and analyze event binding mechanisms for user interactions.

7. AJAX Requests and Fetch API Analysis:

- **Network Traffic Inspection**: Analyze XMLHttpRequest or Fetch API calls to understand data exchanges with the server.
- **Data Format Analysis**: Examine the format of data sent and received in AJAX requests.

8. Asynchronous JavaScript Analysis:

- **Promises and Async/Await**: Analyze the use of Promises and Async/Await for handling asynchronous operations.

- **Callback Analysis**: Understand callback patterns used in asynchronous JavaScript.

9. Security Considerations:

- **Cross-Site Scripting (XSS) Analysis**: Inspect code for potential XSS vulnerabilities and unsafe practices.
- **Content Security Policy (CSP):** Evaluate the implementation of CSP to mitigate XSS risks.
- **Input Validation and Sanitization**: Analyze how user input is validated and sanitized to prevent security issues.

10. Reverse Engineering Obfuscated Code:

- **Obfuscation Techniques**: Identify and understand code obfuscation techniques used to hinder analysis.
- **Deobfuscation Strategies**: Employ deobfuscation techniques to reveal the original code.

11. Performance Optimization Analysis:

- **Code Profiling**: Use profiling tools to identify performance bottlenecks in JavaScript code.
- **Resource Loading Analysis**: Assess how scripts and assets are loaded for optimal performance.

12. Responsive Design and Accessibility Analysis:

- **Media Query Analysis**: Analyze the use of media queries for responsive design.
- **Accessibility Markup**: Check for adherence to accessibility standards and proper use of ARIA roles.

13. Framework and Library-Specific Analysis:

- **Angular, React, or Vue.js Inspection**: Understand the structure and behavior of applications built with specific frameworks.
- **Framework-Specific DevTools**: Use specialized developer tools for frameworks to enhance analysis capabilities.

14. Mobile App JavaScript Analysis:

- **Inspecting Hybrid App Code**: Use tools like Cordova Developer App or WebView debugging for analyzing JavaScript in hybrid mobile apps.
- **React Native Code Inspection**: Analyze React Native JavaScript code for mobile applications.

15. Legal and Ethical Considerations:

- **Compliance with Terms of Service**: Ensure that code analysis activities comply with the terms of service of the web application.
- **Responsible Use**: Use the knowledge gained from code analysis ethically and responsibly, avoiding unauthorized access or misuse.

In conclusion, analyzing JavaScript and front-end code is essential for comprehending the client-side logic of web applications. Adhering to legal and ethical considerations is crucial to ensure responsible and lawful analysis practices.

9.3 Reverse Engineering APIs and Server-side Logic

Reverse engineering APIs and server-side logic is a crucial aspect of understanding how web applications communicate with servers, identifying vulnerabilities, and gaining insights into the backend infrastructure. Here's an exploration of the key aspects involved in reverse engineering APIs and server-side logic:

1. Network Traffic Inspection:

- **Packet Capture**: Use tools like Wireshark to capture and inspect raw network traffic between the client and server.
- **Proxy Servers**: Employ proxy servers like Burp Suite or Charles Proxy to intercept and analyze HTTP(S) requests and responses.

2. API Endpoint Identification:

- **URL and Parameter Analysis**: Identify API endpoints by analyzing URLs and request parameters in intercepted traffic.
- **RESTful API Recognition**: Recognize patterns indicative of RESTful API endpoints.

3. HTTP Methods and Verbs Analysis:

- **HTTP Method Identification**: Determine the HTTP methods (GET, POST, PUT, DELETE, etc.) used by different API endpoints.
- **Verb and Status Code Analysis**: Analyze the use of verbs and HTTP status codes in API responses.

4. Request and Response Structure:

- **Data Format Analysis**: Identify the format of data exchanged in API requests and responses (JSON, XML, etc.).
- **Header Inspection**: Examine headers for authentication tokens, content type, and other relevant information.

5. Authentication Mechanisms:

- **Token Analysis**: Understand how security tokens (JWT, OAuth tokens) are generated, transmitted, and validated.
- **API Key Authentication**: Analyze the use of API keys for authentication and authorization.

6. Session Management:

- **Session Token Analysis**: Investigate how session tokens are managed and validated during API interactions.
- **Stateful and Stateless APIs**: Differentiate between stateful and stateless API interactions.

7. Error Handling Analysis:

- **Error Code Identification**: Identify error codes and messages returned by the API during exceptional scenarios.
- **Security Implications**: Analyze error messages for potential security implications or information leakage.

8. Rate Limiting and Throttling:

- **Rate Limit Analysis**: Identify if the API implements rate limiting to control the number of requests.
- **Throttling Mechanisms:** Analyze mechanisms in place to throttle requests based on frequency or user.

9. Security Headers Analysis:

- **CORS and Security Headers**: Analyze the presence and configuration of Cross-Origin Resource Sharing (CORS) headers, as well as other security headers.
- **Strict-Transport-Security (HSTS):** Evaluate the use of HSTS for enhanced security.

10. Server-side Scripting Languages:

- **Identification of Server-side Code**: Detect server-side scripting languages (PHP, Python, Ruby, etc.) used in API implementations.
- **Code Structure Analysis**: Understand the structure and organization of server-side code.

11. Identifying Third-Party Integrations:

- **API Requests to External Services**: Identify API requests made to external services or third-party APIs.
- **Third-Party Library Recognition**: Recognize third-party libraries used for specific functionalities.

12. Data Storage and Database Interactions:

- **Database Query Analysis**: Identify patterns indicative of database queries within API interactions.
- **Data Storage Mechanisms**: Analyze how data is stored and retrieved from databases.

13. API Versioning and Changes:

- **Version Detection**: Identify API versioning in use and changes between different versions.
- **Handling Deprecated Endpoints**: Analyze how deprecated endpoints are handled in newer API versions.

14. Security Testing and Vulnerability Assessment:

- **Input Validation Analysis**: Assess how input validation is implemented to prevent injection vulnerabilities.
- **Security Misconfigurations**: Identify and test for security misconfigurations in API implementations.
- **Sensitive Data Exposure**: Analyze how sensitive data is handled and ensure proper encryption is in place.

15. Legal and Ethical Considerations:

- **Compliance with Terms of Service**: Ensure that reverse engineering activities comply with the terms of service of the API.
- **Responsible Use**: Use the knowledge gained from API reverse engineering ethically and responsibly, avoiding unauthorized access or misuse.

In conclusion, reverse engineering APIs and server-side logic is crucial for understanding the backend infrastructure of web applications. Adhering to legal and ethical considerations is essential to ensure responsible and lawful reverse engineering practices.

10. Reverse Engineering for Security

Enter the front lines of the digital battlefield as we dive into "Reverse Engineering for Security." In this chapter, we equip you with the skills and strategies needed to identify, exploit, and fortify against vulnerabilities. Uncover the secrets of software defenses, as we guide you through the process of locating and understanding weaknesses within applications and systems. From identifying vulnerabilities through reverse engineering to exploiting security flaws, we provide you with a comprehensive understanding of the offensive and defensive aspects of cybersecurity. Mitigation and prevention strategies become your tools of choice as you navigate the ever-evolving landscape of security challenges. Join us on this chapter where reverse engineering transforms into a powerful weapon for securing digital landscapes, and your expertise becomes a shield against the threats that lurk in the shadows of cyberspace.

10.1 Identifying Software Vulnerabilities

Identifying software vulnerabilities is a critical aspect of reverse engineering, aimed at uncovering weaknesses and security issues within a software system. This process involves a meticulous examination of code, configurations, and interactions to discover potential points of exploitation. Here's an exploration of the key aspects involved in identifying software vulnerabilities:

1. Code Review and Static Analysis:

- **Manual Code Inspection**: Conduct a thorough review of the source code, analyzing each line for security vulnerabilities.

- **Static Analysis Tools**: Utilize automated tools (e.g., static analyzers, linters) to identify common coding mistakes, security issues, and potential vulnerabilities.

2. Input Validation and Injection Points:

- **User Input Analysis**: Examine how user input is handled and validate against potential injection attacks (SQL injection, XSS, etc.).
- **File Upload Security**: Ensure proper validation and security measures for file uploads to prevent malicious file execution.

3. Authentication and Authorization Analysis:

- **Credential Security**: Assess how passwords and sensitive information are stored, transmitted, and validated.
- **Authorization Checks**: Review access control mechanisms to prevent unauthorized access to sensitive functionalities or data.

4. Insecure Direct Object References (IDOR):

- **Data Access Controls**: Analyze how the application controls access to different data objects.
- **URL Parameter Security**: Check for direct object references through URL parameters and validate user permissions.

5. Cryptographic Weaknesses:

- **Encryption Analysis**: Assess the implementation of encryption algorithms and protocols for weaknesses.
- **Key Management**: Review how cryptographic keys are generated, stored, and managed.

6. Security Misconfigurations:

- **Server and Application Configurations**: Examine server settings and application configurations for potential misconfigurations.
- **Default Credentials**: Ensure that default credentials are not present, and access controls are appropriately configured.

7. Cross-Site Scripting (XSS):

- **Code Review for XSS**: Analyze client-side code for instances where user inputs are reflected without proper validation.
- **Context-Aware Output** Encoding: Implement context-aware output encoding to mitigate XSS vulnerabilities.

8. Cross-Site Request Forgery (CSRF):

- **Form Token Usage:** Ensure the use of anti-CSRF tokens in forms to prevent unauthorized actions.
- **CSRF Protection Mechanisms**: Review how the application protects against CSRF attacks.

9. Security Headers Implementation:

- **HTTP Security Headers**: Verify the presence and configuration of security headers (e.g., Content Security Policy, Strict-Transport-Security) for enhanced protection.
- **Referrer Policy**: Evaluate the application's use of referrer policies to control information disclosure.

10. Buffer Overflows and Memory Safety:

- **Code Review for Buffer Overflows**: Analyze code for unsafe buffer operations that could lead to memory overflows.
- **Memory Safety Practices**: Implement secure coding practices to prevent memory-related vulnerabilities.

11. XML External Entity (XXE) Attacks:

- **XML Parsing Security**: Review XML parsing mechanisms for potential vulnerabilities.
- **Disable External Entities**: Disable external entity processing in XML parsers to mitigate XXE attacks.

12. Denial of Service (DoS) Protections:

- **Rate Limiting**: Implement rate limiting to protect against brute force attacks and resource exhaustion.
- **Resource Management**: Analyze how the application handles resource-intensive requests to prevent DoS vulnerabilities.

13. Dynamic Analysis and Penetration Testing:

- **Dynamic Scanning**: Use dynamic analysis tools to simulate real-world attack scenarios and identify vulnerabilities.
- **Penetration Testing**: Conduct ethical hacking to actively test and exploit potential vulnerabilities.

14. Patch Management and Updates:

- **Vulnerability Response**: Establish a process for promptly addressing and patching identified vulnerabilities.
- **Dependency Scanning**: Regularly scan and update third-party libraries and dependencies to address known vulnerabilities.

15. Security Training and Awareness:

- **Developer Training**: Provide security training to developers to enhance their awareness of common vulnerabilities.

- **Code Review Best Practices**: Encourage secure coding practices and conduct regular code reviews for security.

In conclusion, identifying software vulnerabilities requires a comprehensive approach that includes both manual inspection and automated tools. Regular testing, patch management, and a focus on secure coding practices are crucial to maintaining a robust and secure software system.

10.2 Exploiting Security Flaws

Understanding how to exploit security flaws is a crucial aspect of reverse engineering, as it allows security professionals and ethical hackers to simulate real-world attacks and uncover vulnerabilities in software systems. Here's an exploration of key aspects involved in exploiting security flaws:

1. Reconnaissance and Information Gathering:

- **Target Analysis**: Identify the target system, including its architecture, technologies used, and potential entry points.
- **Footprinting**: Gather information about the target's network, infrastructure, and publicly accessible information.

2. Scanning and Enumeration:

- **Port Scanning**: Identify open ports and services running on the target system using tools like Nmap.
- **Service Enumeration**: Gather details about the identified services, versions, and potential vulnerabilities.

3. Vulnerability Identification:

- **Automated Scanning**: Utilize vulnerability scanning tools to identify known vulnerabilities in the target system.
- **Manual Assessment**: Perform manual assessment to discover hidden or complex vulnerabilities that automated tools might miss.

4. Exploitation Techniques:

- **Common Vulnerabilities**: Exploit well-known vulnerabilities, such as SQL injection, cross-site scripting (XSS), or buffer overflows.
- **Zero-Day Exploits**: Develop or use exploits for vulnerabilities that are not yet known to the vendor.

5. Privilege Escalation:

- **User Privilege Analysis**: Exploit weaknesses in user privilege management to escalate privileges.
- **Root/Admin Access**: Gain unauthorized access to privileged accounts for increased control over the target system.

6. Web Application Exploitation:

- **SQL Injection**: Manipulate SQL queries to extract or modify database information.
- **Cross-Site Scripting (XSS):** Inject malicious scripts into web pages to execute unauthorized actions in users' browsers.

7. Network Exploitation:

- **Exploiting Network Protocols**: Target vulnerabilities in network protocols to intercept or manipulate data.

- **Man-in-the-Middle (MitM) Attacks**: Intercept and manipulate communication between entities within the network.

8. Exploiting Buffer Overflows:

- **Identifying Buffer Overflows**: Exploit vulnerabilities in software that allow for buffer overflow attacks.
- **Code Injection**: Inject malicious code into the target system's memory through buffer overflow.

9. Social Engineering:

- **Phishing Attacks**: Exploit human factors through phishing emails or social engineering to gain access credentials.
- **Impersonation**: Pose as a trusted entity to trick users into divulging sensitive information.

10. Post-Exploitation Actions:

- **Data Exfiltration**: Extract sensitive data from the compromised system.
- **Persistence**: Establish backdoors or maintain access for future exploitation.

11. Advanced Persistent Threats (APTs):

- **Stealthy Techniques**: Employ advanced and stealthy techniques to remain undetected within the compromised environment.
- **Long-Term Access**: Maintain persistent access to the target system without raising suspicion.

12. Exploiting Web Services and APIs:

- **API Abuse**: Exploit misconfigurations or vulnerabilities in web services and APIs.
- **XML External Entity (XXE) Attacks**: Leverage XXE vulnerabilities to extract sensitive information.

13. Countermeasures Evasion:

- **Antivirus Bypass**: Evade antivirus detection mechanisms to avoid being flagged during exploitation.
- **Intrusion Detection System (IDS) Evasion**: Use techniques to bypass or disable IDS alerts.

14. Documentation and Reporting:

- **Exploitation Documentation**: Document the steps taken during exploitation, including tools used and outcomes.
- **Vulnerability Report**: Prepare a detailed report outlining the identified vulnerabilities, their severity, and recommended remediation.

15. Ethical Considerations:

- **Responsible Exploitation**: Ensure that exploitation activities are conducted ethically and within the scope of authorized testing.
- **Legal Compliance**: Adhere to legal requirements and obtain proper authorization before engaging in any exploitation activities.

In conclusion, exploiting security flaws requires a deep understanding of vulnerabilities, attack techniques, and the ethical considerations surrounding such activities. Ethical hackers and security professionals leverage this knowledge to help organizations identify and address weaknesses in their systems.

10.3 Mitigating and Preventing Reverse Engineering Attacks

Mitigating and preventing reverse engineering attacks is essential for protecting intellectual property, sensitive information, and the overall security of software systems. Employing effective countermeasures can deter attackers and make it more challenging for them to analyze and exploit software. Here's an exploration of key strategies for mitigating and preventing reverse engineering attacks:

1. Code Obfuscation:

- **Code Transformation**: Use code obfuscation techniques to transform the source code into a more complex and challenging-to-understand form.
- **Symbol Renaming**: Rename variables, functions, and classes to obscure their original purpose.

2. Anti-Debugging Techniques:

- **Debugging Detection**: Implement anti-debugging measures to detect the presence of debugging tools and hinder analysis.
- **Code Traps**: Introduce code traps that trigger when the software is run in a debugger.

3. Binary Protection:

- **Binary Packing**: Employ binary packing techniques to encrypt or compress the executable, making it harder to analyze.
- **Code Encryption**: Encrypt critical parts of the code and decrypt them at runtime to deter static analysis.

4. Tamper Detection and Integrity Checks:

- **Integrity Verification**: Implement checks to verify the integrity of the software at runtime.
- **Tamper Detection**: Detect modifications to the binary or runtime environment, signaling potential tampering.

5. Code Signing:

- **Digital Signatures**: Sign executable files with digital signatures to ensure their authenticity and integrity.
- **Certificate Validation**: Implement checks to validate the authenticity of digital signatures during runtime.

6. Secure Boot and Root of Trust:

- **Secure Boot Mechanisms**: Utilize secure boot processes to ensure that only authenticated and unmodified code is executed.
- **Root of Trust Establishment**: Establish a secure root of trust in hardware or firmware to ensure a trusted execution environment.

7. Hardware-Based Security:

- **Hardware Security Modules (HSMs):** Use dedicated hardware modules for cryptographic operations and key storage.
- **Trusted Execution Environments (TEEs):** Leverage hardware-based TEEs to protect sensitive computations.

8. License Protections and Activation:

- **License Key Mechanisms**: Implement secure license key mechanisms to control software access.

- **Online Activation**: Use online activation processes to verify and validate software licenses.

9. Code Splitting and Dynamic Loading:

- **Dynamic Code Loading**: Load critical parts of the code dynamically at runtime to hinder static analysis.
- **Code Splitting**: Split the code into separate components that interact dynamically, making it more challenging to understand.

10. Runtime Application Self-Protection (RASP):

- **Intrusion Detection**: Implement runtime monitoring to detect and respond to suspicious activities.
- **Dynamic Security Policies**: Adjust security policies based on runtime behavior to adapt to evolving threats.

11. API Security Measures:

- **Authentication and Authorization**: Implement strong authentication and authorization mechanisms for APIs to prevent unauthorized access.
- **API Rate Limiting**: Enforce rate limiting to mitigate abuse and protect against denial-of-service (DoS) attacks.

12. Software Updates and Patch Management:

- **Regular Updates**: Provide regular software updates with security patches to address known vulnerabilities.
- **Automatic Updates**: Implement mechanisms for automatic updates to ensure users have the latest secure versions.

13. Threat Intelligence Integration:

- **Threat Monitoring**: Integrate threat intelligence feeds to stay informed about emerging threats and attack patterns.
- **Anomaly Detection**: Use anomaly detection techniques to identify abnormal behavior indicative of reverse engineering attempts.

14. Legal Protections:

- **Intellectual Property Laws**: Leverage intellectual property laws to protect software assets and take legal action against unauthorized reverse engineering.
- **License Agreements**: Clearly define terms and conditions in license agreements to prohibit reverse engineering.

15. Security Awareness Training:

- **Developer Training**: Provide security training to developers to instill secure coding practices and awareness.
- **User Education**: Educate users about the risks of using tampered or unauthorized software.

In conclusion, a multi-layered approach that combines technical measures, secure coding practices, and legal protections is crucial for effectively mitigating and preventing reverse engineering attacks. Continuous monitoring and adaptation to evolving threats are key components of a robust defense strategy.

11. Legal and Ethical Aspects of Reverse Engineering

Navigate the intricate intersection of technology and law as we delve into the critical domain of "Legal and Ethical Aspects of Reverse Engineering." In this chapter, we shine a spotlight on the ethical considerations and legal ramifications that accompany the art of unraveling digital mysteries. Explore the delicate balance between innovation and intellectual property, dissecting the nuances of copyright issues and navigating the ethical landscape of reverse engineering. We delve into responsible disclosure practices, emphasizing the importance of transparency and collaboration in the digital realm. As you journey through this chapter, you'll gain insights into the ethical considerations that should guide every reverse engineer and the legal frameworks that govern the responsible use of this powerful skill set. Join us on this exploration where legality and ethics converge, offering you the compass to navigate the challenging terrain of responsible reverse engineering.

11.1 Intellectual Property and Copyright Issues

Intellectual property (IP) and copyright issues are significant considerations in the realm of reverse engineering. While reverse engineering itself is a legitimate practice under certain circumstances, it can sometimes raise legal and ethical concerns related to intellectual property rights. Understanding these issues is crucial for practitioners and organizations engaged in reverse engineering activities. Here's an exploration of key aspects related to intellectual property and copyright issues in the context of reverse engineering:

1. Legal Basis for Reverse Engineering:

- **Fair Use Doctrine**: In some jurisdictions, the fair use doctrine may allow for limited reverse engineering for purposes such as research, interoperability, or creating compatible products.
- **Abiding by License Agreements**: Reverse engineering activities should comply with the terms specified in license agreements and any applicable laws.

2. Copyright Protection:

- **Code as Creative Work**: Source code is often considered a creative work and is automatically protected by copyright once created.
- **Expression vs. Functionality**: Copyright protects the expression of ideas but not the functionality itself. Reverse engineering for the purpose of understanding functionality may be permissible.

3. Decompilation and Fair Use:

- **Decompilation Exceptions**: Some jurisdictions provide exceptions for decompilation as part of fair use, particularly for purposes such as interoperability or understanding software behavior.
- **Transformative Use**: Courts may consider whether the decompilation serves a transformative purpose, such as creating a new, interoperable product.

4. Trade Secrets and Reverse Engineering:

- **Trade Secret Protection**: If the information being reverse engineered qualifies as a trade secret, unauthorized reverse engineering may lead to legal consequences.

- **Laws Against Unfair Competition**: Some jurisdictions have laws against unfair competition that may come into play when reverse engineering involves misappropriation of trade secrets.

5. DMCA and Anti-Circumvention Laws:

- **Digital Millennium Copyright Act (DMCA):** The DMCA prohibits the circumvention of technological protection measures (TPMs) used to control access to copyrighted works.
- **Reverse Engineering Exemptions**: The DMCA provides exemptions for reverse engineering activities in certain cases, such as for interoperability or security research.

6. Patent Issues:

- **Patented Software Components**: Reverse engineering patented software components may infringe on patent rights. Patent holders can protect their inventions from being replicated or used without authorization.
- **Patent Exhaustion**: In some jurisdictions, the doctrine of patent exhaustion may limit a patent owner's rights after the first authorized sale of a patented product.

7. Fair Use Factors:

- **Purpose and Character of Use**: Courts consider whether the reverse engineering is transformative or commercial, with transformative uses being more likely to be considered fair.
- **Nature of the Copyrighted Work**: The nature of the copyrighted work and the degree of creativity involved are considered.

- **Amount and Substantiality of Use**: Courts assess the amount and importance of the portion used in relation to the whole.
- **Effect on Market Value**: The potential impact of reverse engineering on the market for the original work is a key factor.

8. Open Source and Copyleft Licenses:

- **Compliance with Licenses**: Reverse engineering activities involving open source or copyleft-licensed software must comply with the terms of those licenses.
- **Copyleft Requirements**: Some licenses, such as the GNU General Public License (GPL), require derivative works to be released under the same license.

9. Case Law Precedents:

- **Court Decisions**: Past court decisions in intellectual property cases involving reverse engineering can provide guidance on legal interpretations and precedents.
- **Jurisdictional Variations**: Laws and court decisions may vary by jurisdiction, and practitioners should be aware of regional nuances.

10. Ethical Considerations:

- **Responsible Use**: Even if legally permissible, practitioners should consider the ethical implications of their reverse engineering activities.
- **Respecting IP Rights**: Practitioners should respect the intellectual property rights of others and avoid activities that could lead to unfair competition or unauthorized use.

Navigating intellectual property and copyright issues in reverse engineering requires a nuanced understanding of legal frameworks, licenses, and ethical considerations. Practitioners and organizations should seek legal advice when uncertain about the legality of specific reverse engineering activities and strive to operate within the bounds of applicable laws and regulations.

11.2 Ethical Considerations in Reverse Engineering

Reverse engineering, while a valuable and sometimes necessary practice, raises ethical considerations that practitioners should carefully navigate. Ethical behavior in reverse engineering is essential to ensure responsible conduct, respect for intellectual property, and avoidance of harm. Here's an exploration of key ethical considerations in the field of reverse engineering:

1. Authorization and Legality:

- **Obtaining Consent**: Obtain proper authorization from the software owner or authorized party before engaging in reverse engineering activities.
- **Compliance with Laws**: Ensure that reverse engineering activities comply with applicable laws, including intellectual property laws and anti-circumvention regulations.

2. Purpose and Intent:

- **Ethical Purpose**: Conduct reverse engineering for ethical purposes, such as improving interoperability, achieving compatibility, or conducting security research.
- **Avoiding Malicious Intent**: Refrain from reverse engineering with malicious intent, such as creating unauthorized copies, competing unfairly, or engaging in industrial espionage.

3. Responsible Disclosure:

- **Security Vulnerabilities**: If security vulnerabilities are discovered during reverse engineering, follow responsible disclosure practices by notifying the software owner or relevant stakeholders.
- **Collaboration with Vendors**: Collaborate with software vendors to address vulnerabilities and contribute to the improvement of security measures.

4. Protection of Intellectual Property:

- **Respect for IP Rights**: Respect the intellectual property rights of others, including copyrights, patents, and trade secrets.
- **Avoiding Unauthorized Use**: Do not use reverse-engineered information for unauthorized purposes, such as creating competing products without proper authorization.

5. Transparency and Honesty:

- **Transparent Practices**: Be transparent about the purpose and scope of reverse engineering activities, especially when collaborating with others.
- **Honest Representation**: Provide accurate and honest representations of findings, avoiding exaggerations or misrepresentations.

6. Minimization of Harm:

- **Avoiding Harmful Actions**: Refrain from actions that may harm individuals, organizations, or the public as a result of reverse engineering activities.

- **Consideration of Consequences**: Consider the potential consequences of reverse engineering, including unintended negative impacts.

7. Ethical Use of Findings:

- **Responsible Application**: Use the knowledge gained from reverse engineering ethically and responsibly, ensuring that it is applied for positive and constructive purposes.
- **Avoiding Unfair Advantage**: Avoid using reverse-engineered information to gain an unfair advantage or to engage in activities that undermine fair competition.

8. Privacy Considerations:

- **User Privacy**: Consider and respect user privacy when conducting reverse engineering activities, particularly when analyzing applications that handle personal or sensitive data.
- **Data Protection Laws**: Adhere to data protection laws and regulations when reverse engineering involves the analysis of personal information.

9. Collaboration and Information Sharing:

- **Collaboration Ethics**: Collaborate with other researchers and stakeholders in an ethical manner, sharing information responsibly.
- **Avoiding Plagiarism**: Give proper credit to the work of others and avoid plagiarism when disseminating findings.

10. Continuous Learning and Professionalism:

- **Professional Development**: Stay informed about evolving ethical standards, legal requirements, and best practices in reverse engineering.

- **Professionalism**: Conduct reverse engineering activities with a high level of professionalism, respecting the norms and standards of the cybersecurity and software development communities.

11. Public Interest Considerations:

- **Balancing Public Interest**: Consider the broader public interest when engaging in reverse engineering, particularly in cases where security vulnerabilities may impact a large number of users.
- **Advocacy for Responsible Practices**: Advocate for responsible reverse engineering practices within the community and industry.

12. Ethical Decision-Making Framework:

- **Ethical Frameworks**: Use ethical decision-making frameworks to guide complex decisions in situations where ethical considerations are paramount.
- **Consultation with Peers**: Seek input and guidance from peers, mentors, or ethical committees when facing ethical dilemmas.

Navigating ethical considerations in reverse engineering requires a commitment to responsible conduct, a strong ethical framework, and continuous self-reflection. Practitioners should be proactive in addressing ethical challenges and contribute to the development of ethical norms within the field.

11.3 Responsible Disclosure Practices

Responsible disclosure is a crucial aspect of ethical behavior in the realm of cybersecurity and reverse engineering. It involves reporting security vulnerabilities and findings to the affected parties in a responsible and coordinated manner, allowing them to address and remediate the issues. Here's an exploration of key principles and practices associated with responsible disclosure:

1. Identification of Security Vulnerabilities:

- **Thorough Analysis**: Conduct a thorough analysis to identify and understand security vulnerabilities within software or systems.
- **Scope Definition**: Clearly define the scope of the vulnerabilities, including affected components and potential impact.

2. Contacting the Software Vendor or Owner:

- **Direct Communication**: Establish direct communication with the software vendor or owner as soon as security vulnerabilities are identified.
- **Notification Channels**: Use official and secure channels for communication, such as security@domain.com or other designated contact points.

3. Providing Detailed Information:

- **Comprehensive Report**: Prepare a comprehensive and clear report detailing the identified vulnerabilities, including their nature, potential impact, and any relevant technical details.
- **Reproduction Steps**: Include detailed steps to reproduce the vulnerabilities, aiding the vendor in understanding and validating the findings.

4. Setting a Disclosure Timeline:

- **Mutual Agreement**: Work with the software vendor to set a mutually agreed-upon timeline for disclosing the vulnerabilities.
- **Reasonable Timeframe**: Allow the vendor a reasonable amount of time to assess, validate, and address the vulnerabilities before public disclosure.

5. Coordinated Release of Information:

- **Coordinated Public Disclosure**: Aim for a coordinated release of information, where the disclosure of the vulnerabilities is made simultaneously by both the security researcher and the vendor.
- **Minimizing Risk**: Coordinated disclosure helps minimize the risk of exploitation before patches or mitigations are available.

6. Acknowledgment and Recognition:

- **Acknowledgment of Contributors**: Software vendors should acknowledge and recognize the contribution of security researchers in discovering and reporting vulnerabilities.
- **CVE Assignments**: Ensure that Common Vulnerabilities and Exposures (CVE) identifiers are assigned to the reported vulnerabilities.

7. Confidentiality and Non-Disclosure Agreements:

- **Confidentiality Agreements**: If requested by the vendor, consider entering into confidentiality or non-disclosure agreements to protect sensitive information.
- **Respecting Vendor Requests**: Respect any reasonable requests from the vendor regarding the timing and content of disclosure.

8. Continuous Communication:

- **Regular Updates**: Maintain regular communication with the software vendor to receive updates on the progress of vulnerability remediation efforts.
- **Mutual Collaboration**: Foster a collaborative relationship between security researchers and vendors to enhance overall cybersecurity.

9. Offering Guidance on Mitigations:

- **Mitigation Suggestions**: Provide suggestions or temporary mitigations that can help the vendor and users protect themselves while a permanent fix is being developed.
- **Cooperative Problem-Solving**: Engage in cooperative problem-solving discussions to explore effective solutions.

10. Responsible Public Disclosure:

- **Publicly Acknowledge Fixes**: Once the vendor has released patches or mitigations, publicly acknowledge their efforts in addressing the vulnerabilities.
- **Educational Content**: Consider providing educational content alongside public disclosures to raise awareness about the importance of software security.

11. Collaboration with Security Communities:

- **Sharing Information**: Share relevant information with security communities, forums, or organizations to contribute to the collective knowledge and awareness.
- **Community Collaboration**: Encourage collaboration within the security community to address broader cybersecurity challenges.

12. Legal and Ethical Considerations:

- **Adherence to Laws**: Ensure that responsible disclosure practices adhere to applicable laws and regulations, respecting legal considerations.
- **Ethical Conduct**: Uphold ethical standards throughout the disclosure process, demonstrating integrity and responsible behavior.

By following responsible disclosure practices, security researchers and practitioners contribute to the overall improvement of software security while minimizing the risk of harm to users and organizations. This collaborative approach fosters a more secure and resilient cybersecurity landscape.

12. Case Studies in Reverse Engineering

Embark on a fascinating exploration of real-world challenges and triumphs as we delve into "Case Studies in Reverse Engineering." In this chapter, we present a collection of compelling stories and practical examples that showcase the diverse applications and impact of reverse engineering across various industries. Dive deep into the intricacies of successful reverse engineering projects, learning valuable lessons from notable cases. From unraveling complex software protections to exposing vulnerabilities in critical systems, each case study provides a window into the problem-solving prowess of reverse engineers. As you journey through this chapter, you'll gain a nuanced understanding of how reverse engineering techniques can be applied to address practical challenges and shape the technological landscape. Join us in this chapter where theory meets reality, and the art of breaking transforms into a powerful tool for innovation and problem-solving.

12.1 Real-world Examples of Successful Reverse Engineering

Reverse engineering has played a crucial role in uncovering vulnerabilities, understanding complex systems, and advancing technological innovation. Here are some real-world examples where successful reverse engineering efforts have made a significant impact:

Stuxnet Worm (2010):

- **Context**: Stuxnet is a sophisticated computer worm that targeted supervisory control and data acquisition (SCADA) systems, specifically those used in Iran's nuclear program.
- **Reverse Engineering Impact**: Security researchers, including those at Symantec and Kaspersky, played a vital role in reverse engineering Stuxnet to understand its capabilities and the specific targeting of industrial control systems.

Sony PlayStation (Various Models):

- **Context**: Over the years, hackers and modders have successfully reverse engineered several generations of Sony PlayStation consoles to run unauthorized software, homebrew applications, and pirated games.
- **Reverse Engineering Impact**: This has led to a vibrant homebrew community, but it also raised concerns about piracy and forced Sony to continually update its security measures.

Apple iOS Jailbreaking:

- **Context**: Jailbreaking involves removing software restrictions on Apple's iOS operating system to install apps and modifications not approved by Apple.
- **Reverse Engineering Impact**: Jailbreaking efforts have successfully reverse engineered iOS to allow greater customization and third-party app installations. Apple, in response, has continued to enhance iOS security.

Car Key Fob Cloning:

- **Context**: Researchers have demonstrated the ability to reverse engineer and clone the signals from car key fobs, allowing unauthorized access to vehicles.

- **Reverse Engineering Impact**: Car manufacturers improved the security of keyless entry systems after such vulnerabilities were exposed, showcasing the importance of reverse engineering in enhancing automotive security.

Intel x86 Architecture:

- **Context**: The x86 architecture used in Intel processors is proprietary, but its details have been reverse engineered over the years.
- **Reverse Engineering Impact**: This reverse engineering has enabled the development of alternative operating systems (such as Linux) and open-source compilers compatible with Intel processors, fostering innovation and competition.

Adobe Flash Player Vulnerabilities:

- **Context**: Over the years, security researchers have discovered and analyzed vulnerabilities in Adobe Flash Player, a widely used multimedia platform.
- **Reverse Engineering Impact**: Identifying and understanding these vulnerabilities through reverse engineering has been crucial for developing patches and securing systems against potential exploits.

Modding and Custom Firmware for Game Consoles:

- **Context**: Enthusiasts have successfully reverse engineered and created custom firmware for game consoles like the Nintendo Wii and Sony PlayStation Portable (PSP).
- **Reverse Engineering Impact**: These efforts have led to homebrew communities, expanded functionalities, and the preservation of older gaming systems beyond their original capabilities.

DLL Injection and Game Hacking:

- **Context**: Reverse engineering has been used in the gaming community to understand and modify the behavior of games through techniques like DLL injection.
- **Reverse Engineering Impact**: Game hackers use reverse engineering to discover vulnerabilities, create cheats, and develop mods. Game developers respond by improving anti-cheat measures and security.

Wireless Router Firmware Modifications:

- **Context**: Enthusiasts and security researchers have reverse engineered and modified the firmware of wireless routers to add features or address security issues.
- **Reverse Engineering Impact**: These efforts have contributed to the development of alternative firmware like OpenWrt, providing users with more control over their router's functionality and security.

Cryptocurrency Protocol Analysis:

- **Context**: Researchers have reverse engineered and analyzed various cryptocurrency protocols, including Bitcoin and Ethereum.
- **Reverse Engineering Impact**: Understanding these protocols through reverse engineering has led to improvements in security, the discovery of vulnerabilities, and the development of new blockchain technologies.

These examples highlight the diverse applications of reverse engineering, ranging from security research and vulnerability discovery to the modification of consumer electronics and the advancement of open-source initiatives. While reverse engineering can raise ethical and legal considerations, it remains a valuable tool for understanding and improving complex systems.

12.2 Lessons Learned from Notable Cases

Several notable reverse engineering cases have provided valuable lessons for cybersecurity, technology, and legal communities. Examining these cases offers insights into the challenges, consequences, and advancements related to reverse engineering. Here are lessons learned from some prominent cases:

Sony BMG Rootkit Scandal (2005):

- **Lesson**: Transparency and Accountability are Critical.
- **Background**: Sony BMG's attempt to prevent unauthorized copying of CDs involved installing a rootkit on users' computers without proper disclosure.
- **Outcome**: This case highlighted the importance of transparency, user consent, and accountability in the deployment of digital rights management (DRM) technologies.

Apple vs. FBI iPhone Encryption Case (2016):

- **Lesson**: Balancing Security and Privacy is a Complex Challenge.
- **Background**: The FBI sought Apple's assistance in unlocking an iPhone related to a terrorism investigation, sparking a debate on privacy, security, and government access to encrypted devices.
- **Outcome**: The case emphasized the challenges of finding a balance between privacy rights and law enforcement needs, highlighting the broader implications of encryption and security measures.

Microsoft vs. Motorola (2012):

- **Lesson**: Standards Essential Patents (SEPs) Require Fair, Reasonable, and Non-Discriminatory (FRAND) Licensing.
- **Background**: Microsoft and Motorola engaged in legal battles over SEPs related to industry standards for video compression and wireless technologies.
- **Outcome**: Courts emphasized the importance of adhering to FRAND licensing terms for SEPs to ensure fair competition and avoid anticompetitive practices.

Oracle vs. Google (2010-2021):

- **Lesson**: API Copyright and Fair Use are Key Legal Considerations.
- **Background**: Oracle claimed copyright infringement when Google used Java APIs in Android. The case went through multiple trials and appeals.
- **Outcome**: The legal battles underscored the complexities of API copyright and the application of fair use, impacting the software development community and API usage considerations.

Volkswagen Emissions Scandal (2015):

- **Lesson**: Reverse Engineering can Expose Corporate Wrongdoing.
- **Background**: Researchers discovered that Volkswagen manipulated emissions tests using software on certain diesel engines.
- **Outcome**: The case highlighted the role of reverse engineering in uncovering corporate misconduct, emphasizing the need for transparency and ethical behavior in the automotive industry.

Epic Games vs. Apple (2020):

- **Lesson**: App Store Practices and Monopoly Concerns.

- **Background**: Epic Games challenged Apple's App Store policies, leading to the removal of Fortnite from the App Store.
- **Outcome**: The case raised questions about app store practices, antitrust concerns, and the need for fair competition in the digital ecosystem.

Equifax Data Breach (2017):

- **Lesson**: Cybersecurity Vulnerabilities Have Far-reaching Consequences.
- **Background**: Equifax suffered a massive data breach due to unpatched software, exposing sensitive information of millions of consumers.
- **Outcome**: The case underscored the importance of promptly addressing cybersecurity vulnerabilities and implementing robust security measures to protect user data.

SolarWinds Cyberattack (2020):

- **Lesson**: Software Supply Chain Security is Critical.
- **Background**: The SolarWinds cyberattack compromised the software supply chain, leading to widespread cybersecurity breaches.
- **Outcome**: The incident highlighted the need for enhanced supply chain security practices and vigilance in defending against sophisticated attacks on software vendors.

Qualcomm vs. Apple (2017):

- **Lesson**: Patent Disputes Can Impact Innovation and Consumer Choices.
- **Background**: Qualcomm and Apple engaged in legal battles over patent licensing fees and technology used in iPhones.
- **Outcome**: The case illustrated how patent disputes can impact technological innovation, product development, and

consumer choices, emphasizing the importance of fair competition.

TikTok Ban and Oracle-Walmart Deal (2020):

- **Lesson**: National Security Concerns Impact Technology Business.
- **Background**: The U.S. government raised national security concerns over TikTok's Chinese ownership, leading to proposed bans and discussions about potential partnerships.
- **Outcome**: The case highlighted the intersection of national security, technology, and international business, showcasing the complexities of geopolitical considerations.

These cases demonstrate the multifaceted nature of reverse engineering's impact on technology, security, law, and society. They emphasize the need for ethical conduct, transparent practices, and a balanced approach to addressing challenges in the rapidly evolving landscape of technology and cybersecurity.

12.3 Practical Applications in Various Industries

Reverse engineering is a versatile tool with applications across various industries, enabling innovation, troubleshooting, and improvement of existing products and systems. Here are practical applications of reverse engineering in different sectors:

Automotive Industry:

- **Component Analysis**: Reverse engineering is used to analyze and understand the components of automotive systems, such as engines, transmissions, and electronic control units (ECUs).

- **Performance Enhancement**: Automotive enthusiasts use reverse engineering to modify and enhance vehicle performance, including engine tuning and aftermarket part integration.
- **Legacy Parts Replication**: When original parts are no longer available, reverse engineering allows for the reproduction of legacy components.

Aerospace and Defense:

- **Aircraft Maintenance**: Reverse engineering supports the maintenance of aging aircraft by recreating obsolete or hard-to-find parts.
- **Aircraft Upgrades**: Upgrading avionics systems and components through reverse engineering ensures compatibility with modern technologies.
- **Military Hardware Analysis**: Understanding and analyzing foreign military hardware through reverse engineering can provide valuable intelligence.

Consumer Electronics:

- **Product Design**: Reverse engineering is employed to analyze competitors' products, inspiring the design of new consumer electronics with improved features.
- **Repair and Maintenance**: Technicians use reverse engineering to troubleshoot and repair electronic devices, especially when official repair manuals or spare parts are not available.
- **Firmware Analysis**: Reverse engineering helps uncover vulnerabilities in firmware and improve the security of consumer electronics.

Medical Devices:

- **Implantable Devices**: Reverse engineering is applied to medical implants and devices to understand their functionality and improve upon existing designs.
- **Custom Prosthetics**: Tailoring prosthetic devices to individual patients often involves reverse engineering to create personalized and comfortable solutions.
- **Legacy Device Support**: When manufacturers discontinue medical devices, reverse engineering can be used to extend the life of existing equipment by replicating essential components.

Information Technology and Cybersecurity:

- **Malware Analysis**: Security researchers use reverse engineering to analyze and understand the behavior of malware, aiding in the development of countermeasures.
- **Software Patching**: Reverse engineering helps identify vulnerabilities in software, enabling the development of patches to improve security.
- **Legacy Software Support**: When source code is unavailable, reverse engineering can be used to understand and extend the functionality of legacy software.

Oil and Gas Industry:

- **Equipment Maintenance**: Reverse engineering supports the maintenance of critical machinery in the oil and gas sector, ensuring the availability of spare parts.
- **Pipeline Analysis**: Understanding the design and specifications of existing pipelines through reverse engineering aids in planning and maintenance activities.
- **Safety Enhancements**: Reverse engineering helps improve safety features in equipment and systems used in oil and gas operations.

Electrical and Electronic Components:

- **Integrated Circuits (ICs):** Reverse engineering is used to understand the internal structure of ICs, facilitating the development of compatible or improved versions.
- **Printed Circuit Board (PCB) Analysis:** Reverse engineering PCBs helps diagnose faults, optimize layouts, and enhance electronic designs.
- **Legacy System Integration:** Reverse engineering enables the integration of modern electronic components with legacy systems, extending their operational life.

Architectural Preservation:

- **Historical Buildings:** Reverse engineering aids in the restoration and preservation of historical buildings by recreating architectural details and decorative elements.
- **Artifacts Replication:** In the restoration of cultural artifacts, reverse engineering can be employed to replicate missing or damaged components with precision.
- **Digital Archiving:** Creating digital models through reverse engineering ensures the documentation and preservation of architectural heritage.

Footwear and Fashion Industry:

- **Product Design:** Reverse engineering assists in understanding the design and manufacturing processes of competitor products, inspiring new footwear designs.
- **Custom Shoe Manufacturing:** Personalized and custom-fit shoes are made possible by reverse engineering the geometry of individuals' feet.
- **Material Analysis:** Reverse engineering supports the analysis of materials used in footwear, contributing to the development of more comfortable and durable products.

Manufacturing and Production:

- **Tooling and Molds**: Reverse engineering is utilized in the reproduction of tooling and molds for manufacturing processes.
- **Quality Control**: Reverse engineering helps analyze and ensure the quality of competitor products, aiding in the improvement of manufacturing processes.
- **Process Optimization**: Studying and understanding manufacturing processes through reverse engineering enables optimization for efficiency and cost-effectiveness.

These practical applications demonstrate the wide-ranging impact of reverse engineering in enhancing product development, maintenance, and innovation across diverse industries. As technology continues to advance, the role of reverse engineering in problem-solving and improvement is likely to expand even further.

13. Future Trends in Reverse Engineering

Peer into the crystal ball of technology as we explore "Future Trends in Reverse Engineering." In this chapter, we navigate the rapidly evolving landscape of the digital frontier, anticipating the emerging technologies and challenges that will shape the future of reverse engineering. From the rise of new tools and methodologies to the integration of artificial intelligence and machine learning, we delve into the cutting-edge trends that will redefine the boundaries of this captivating discipline. As we explore the challenges and opportunities on the horizon, you'll gain insights into the role of reverse engineering in shaping the security, innovation, and sustainability of tomorrow's technologies. Join us on this journey into the future, where the art of breaking becomes a dynamic force driving progress in the ever-evolving world of reverse engineering.

13.1 Emerging Technologies in Reverse Engineering

As technology evolves, new tools and techniques continue to emerge in the field of reverse engineering, enhancing the capabilities of researchers, developers, and security professionals. Here are some emerging technologies that are shaping the landscape of reverse engineering:

Machine Learning and AI:

- **Application**: Machine learning and artificial intelligence are being applied to automate aspects of reverse engineering, such as pattern recognition, code analysis, and vulnerability detection.

- **Benefits**: These technologies can speed up the analysis process, identify complex patterns in large datasets, and enhance the detection of anomalies and potential security threats.

Interactive Disassemblers:

- **Application**: Interactive disassemblers, like Binary Ninja and Cutter, provide dynamic and collaborative environments for reverse engineers to analyze and manipulate binary code.
- **Benefits**: These tools offer user-friendly interfaces, real-time collaboration features, and scripting capabilities, making reverse engineering more accessible and efficient.

Fuzzing Techniques:

- **Application**: Fuzz testing involves inputting large amounts of random or unexpected data to find vulnerabilities in software. Recent advances in fuzzing techniques, such as AFL (American Fuzzy Lop) and libFuzzer, enhance the automation of this process.
- **Benefits**: Fuzzing helps uncover security vulnerabilities, improve software robustness, and identify potential attack vectors by generating diverse input scenarios.

Symbolic Execution:

- **Application**: Symbolic execution allows the analysis of code paths with symbolic values instead of concrete inputs, enabling the exploration of multiple execution paths without specific inputs.
- **Benefits**: This technique aids in identifying complex vulnerabilities, understanding program behavior under various conditions, and enhancing code coverage during analysis.

Dynamic Binary Translation:

- **Application**: Dynamic Binary Translation (DBT) technologies, such as QEMU, enable the execution of binaries on different architectures, facilitating cross-platform analysis.
- **Benefits**: DBT is valuable for analyzing software on diverse platforms without access to native hardware, making it easier to study and understand the behavior of applications.

Memory Forensics:

- **Application**: Memory forensics involves analyzing the contents of a system's memory to extract information about running processes, network connections, and potential security threats.
- **Benefits**: This technique is crucial for investigating cyber incidents, identifying malware, and understanding the runtime behavior of applications.

Binary Diffing:

- **Application**: Binary diffing tools, like BinDiff, compare different versions of binary files to identify changes and similarities.
- **Benefits**: Binary diffing is used for analyzing software updates, identifying security patches, and understanding the impact of code changes between versions.

Hardware-Assisted Techniques:

- **Application**: Hardware-assisted reverse engineering tools, such as JTAG interfaces and hardware debuggers, provide low-level access to embedded systems and integrated circuits.

- **Benefits**: These tools enable direct interaction with hardware components, facilitating the analysis of firmware, embedded systems, and IoT devices.

Augmented Reality (AR):

- **Application**: AR technologies are increasingly used in reverse engineering for visualizing and interacting with 3D models of physical objects and components.
- **Benefits**: AR enhances the understanding of complex structures, facilitates collaborative analysis, and provides immersive experiences for reverse engineers working on physical products.

Blockchain Analysis:

- **Application**: With the rise of blockchain technologies, reverse engineering is applied to analyze smart contracts, identify vulnerabilities, and understand the behavior of decentralized applications (DApps).
- **Benefits**: Blockchain analysis helps ensure the security and reliability of smart contracts, uncover vulnerabilities, and enhance the overall robustness of blockchain-based systems.

These emerging technologies are driving innovation in the field of reverse engineering, making it more efficient, accessible, and powerful. As the complexity of software and hardware systems continues to grow, staying abreast of these technological advancements becomes essential for professionals in the reverse engineering space.

13.2 Challenges and Opportunities

Reverse engineering, while a powerful and indispensable practice, is not without its challenges. However, these challenges also present opportunities for innovation and improvement within the field. Here are some key challenges and corresponding opportunities in reverse engineering:

Challenges:

Code Obfuscation and Anti-Analysis Techniques:

- **Challenge**: Increasingly sophisticated code obfuscation and anti-analysis techniques make it challenging to understand and analyze software.
- **Opportunity**: Development of advanced analysis tools and techniques, including machine learning algorithms, to counteract obfuscation and identify anti-analysis measures.

Lack of Documentation and Source Code:

- **Challenge**: Reverse engineers often work without access to proper documentation or the original source code, making the analysis more challenging.
- **Opportunity**: Development of methods for reverse engineering that are less dependent on the availability of documentation, such as improved dynamic analysis and behavior-based techniques.

Legal and Ethical Considerations:

- **Challenge**: Reverse engineering can raise legal and ethical concerns, especially when it involves proprietary software or intellectual property.
- **Opportunity**: Advocacy for clearer legal frameworks, industry standards, and ethical guidelines to navigate the complex landscape of reverse engineering responsibly.

Rapidly Evolving Technologies:

- **Challenge**: The rapid pace of technological advancement requires reverse engineers to continually update their skills and tools.
- **Opportunity**: Establishment of continuous learning initiatives, collaborative knowledge-sharing platforms, and professional development programs to keep practitioners abreast of emerging technologies.

Hardware-Level Reverse Engineering:

- **Challenge**: Analyzing and understanding complex integrated circuits and hardware systems pose unique challenges in terms of accessibility and expertise.
- **Opportunity**: Development of advanced hardware-assisted reverse engineering tools, educational programs, and collaborative efforts to address challenges associated with hardware analysis.

Resource Intensiveness:

- **Challenge**: Reverse engineering can be resource-intensive, requiring significant time and computational power, especially for large and complex systems.
- **Opportunity**: Optimization of analysis tools, parallelization of tasks, and advancements in hardware capabilities to enhance the efficiency of reverse engineering processes.

Opportunities:

Automation and Machine Learning:

Opportunity: Integration of automation and machine learning in reverse engineering processes to accelerate analysis, identify patterns, and automate repetitive tasks.

Collaborative Platforms:

Opportunity: Development of collaborative platforms that facilitate knowledge-sharing, resource pooling, and collective problem-solving within the reverse engineering community.

Interdisciplinary Collaboration:

Opportunity: Encouraging collaboration between reverse engineers, cybersecurity experts, legal professionals, and industry stakeholders to address challenges holistically.

Open Source Tools and Knowledge:

Opportunity: Emphasis on open source tools and the sharing of knowledge to create a more transparent and collaborative reverse engineering ecosystem.

Security Education and Awareness:

Opportunity: Increased focus on security education and awareness programs to educate developers, engineers, and stakeholders about the importance of secure coding practices and the role of reverse engineering in enhancing cybersecurity.

Ethical Hacking and Bug Bounty Programs:

Opportunity: Expansion of ethical hacking initiatives and bug bounty programs, encouraging responsible disclosure of vulnerabilities and fostering a positive relationship between security researchers and software vendors.

Regulatory Frameworks:

Opportunity: Advocacy for the development of regulatory frameworks that balance the interests of intellectual property protection and the legitimate use of reverse engineering for security and innovation.

Continual Professional Development:

Opportunity: Establishment of structured professional development programs, certifications, and training courses to ensure that reverse engineers stay current with evolving technologies and best practices.

Addressing these challenges and embracing the opportunities in reverse engineering requires a collective effort from the community, industry, and policymakers. By fostering innovation, collaboration, and responsible practices, the field of reverse engineering can continue to play a vital role in advancing technology and cybersecurity.

13.3 The Evolving Landscape of Reverse Engineering

The landscape of reverse engineering is dynamic, shaped by technological advancements, cybersecurity challenges, and the continuous evolution of software and hardware systems. Several key trends contribute to the changing nature of reverse engineering:

Increased Complexity of Software:

- **Trend**: Software systems are becoming more complex, incorporating advanced encryption, anti-analysis techniques, and intricate architectures.

- **Impact**: Reverse engineers must adapt by developing advanced skills, leveraging automation, and exploring new methodologies to analyze and understand complex software structures.

Rise of Machine Learning in Analysis:

- **Trend**: The integration of machine learning and artificial intelligence in reverse engineering tools and processes is gaining prominence.
- **Impact**: Machine learning enhances the speed and accuracy of analysis, aids in identifying patterns, and automates certain aspects of reverse engineering tasks.

Shift Toward Behavioral Analysis:

- **Trend**: There is a growing emphasis on behavioral analysis, focusing on the runtime behavior of software and malware.
- **Impact**: Behavioral analysis provides insights into dynamic aspects, aiding in the detection of evasive techniques and zero-day vulnerabilities that may go unnoticed in static analysis.

Hardware and Firmware Challenges:

- **Trend**: With the proliferation of embedded systems, IoT devices, and proprietary hardware, reverse engineering is extending beyond software to encompass hardware and firmware analysis.
- **Impact**: Reverse engineers need to acquire expertise in hardware-level analysis, utilizing tools like JTAG interfaces and hardware debuggers to understand the intricacies of integrated circuits.

Ethical Considerations and Responsible Disclosure:

- **Trend**: The importance of ethical conduct and responsible disclosure in reverse engineering is gaining recognition.
- **Impact**: Legal and ethical considerations are shaping the practices of security researchers, emphasizing responsible disclosure, adherence to laws, and ethical behavior throughout the analysis process.

Cross-Disciplinary Collaboration:

- **Trend**: There is a trend toward increased collaboration between reverse engineers, cybersecurity experts, legal professionals, and industry stakeholders.
- **Impact**: Cross-disciplinary collaboration fosters a holistic approach to addressing challenges, incorporating diverse perspectives, and finding comprehensive solutions

Integration of Augmented Reality:

- **Trend**: Augmented reality technologies are being integrated into reverse engineering processes for enhanced visualization and interaction with 3D models.
- **Impact**: Augmented reality provides an immersive experience, facilitating the analysis of physical objects, architectural structures, and mechanical components.

Community-Driven Knowledge Sharing:

- **Trend**: The reverse engineering community is actively engaged in knowledge sharing through open source tools, collaborative platforms, and educational initiatives.
- **Impact**: Community-driven knowledge sharing accelerates skill development, facilitates resource pooling, and creates a supportive ecosystem for both experienced practitioners and newcomers.

Focus on Supply Chain Security:

- **Trend**: In the wake of high-profile supply chain attacks, there is a growing emphasis on supply chain security, including the analysis of software and firmware within the supply chain.
- **Impact**: Reverse engineers play a crucial role in identifying vulnerabilities, ensuring the integrity of software components, and enhancing overall supply chain resilience.

Continuous Professional Development:

- **Trend**: Recognizing the need for continual learning, professionals in reverse engineering are actively pursuing ongoing education and certifications.
- **Impact**: Continuous professional development ensures that practitioners stay abreast of emerging technologies, industry trends, and evolving best practices.

The evolving landscape of reverse engineering reflects the dynamic nature of technology and the cybersecurity landscape. As the field continues to adapt to new challenges and opportunities, practitioners must stay vigilant, continually update their skill sets, and embrace collaborative approaches to effectively navigate the complexities of reverse engineering.

14. Building a Career in Reverse Engineering

Embark on a strategic exploration of professional growth and expertise as we delve into "Building a Career in Reverse Engineering." In this chapter, we guide you through the process of cultivating the skills and knowledge needed to thrive in the dynamic field of reverse engineering. From developing a strong foundation in the fundamentals to honing specialized expertise, we map out a pathway for both aspiring enthusiasts and seasoned professionals. Explore the diverse job opportunities and industries where reverse engineering plays a pivotal role, and learn the art of continuous learning and professional development. As you navigate through this chapter, you'll discover the keys to building a fulfilling and impactful career in reverse engineering, where your skills become a catalyst for innovation and problem-solving. Join us in this exploration of the pathways to success in a field where the art of breaking transforms into a rewarding and dynamic profession.

14.1 Developing Skills and Expertise

Developing expertise in reverse engineering requires a combination of theoretical knowledge, practical experience, and a commitment to staying updated on emerging technologies. Here are steps and recommendations for aspiring reverse engineers to build and enhance their skills:

Understand the Basics:

- **Computer Architecture**: Gain a solid understanding of computer architecture, including the CPU, memory, registers, and basic assembly language.

- **Programming Languages**: Familiarize yourself with programming languages commonly used in reverse engineering, such as C and Python.

Learn Assembly Language:

- **x86 and x64 Architecture**: Master assembly languages, particularly for x86 and x64 architectures, as they are prevalent in reverse engineering tasks.
- **Instruction Set:** Understand common assembly instructions, registers, and memory addressing modes.

Explore Operating Systems:

- **Windows and Linux**: Acquire knowledge of both Windows and Linux operating systems, as they are commonly encountered in reverse engineering scenarios.
- **System Calls and API**: Understand system calls, API functions, and libraries used by operating systems.

Build Programming Skills:

- **Scripting Languages**: Develop proficiency in scripting languages like Python, which is widely used for automating tasks and creating analysis tools.
- **Debugging Skills**: Learn debugging techniques using tools like GDB, WinDbg, or OllyDbg to analyze program execution.

Study Cryptography:

- **Cryptography Fundamentals**: Understand the basics of cryptography, as encryption and decryption mechanisms are often encountered in reverse engineering.
- **Common Algorithms**: Familiarize yourself with common cryptographic algorithms and protocols.

Gain Proficiency in Tools:

- **Disassemblers**: Learn to use popular disassemblers such as IDA Pro, Ghidra, and Radare2 for analyzing binary code.
- **Debuggers**: Develop skills in using debuggers like GDB, WinDbg, and OllyDbg for dynamic analysis.
- **Hex Editors**: Become proficient in hex editors for manual inspection and manipulation of binary files.

Explore Reverse Engineering Frameworks:

- **Binary Ninja, Cutter, and Angr**: Familiarize yourself with newer frameworks like Binary Ninja, Cutter, and Angr that offer modern and interactive reverse engineering environments.

Participate in Capture The Flag (CTF) Challenges:

- **CTF Platforms**: Engage in CTF challenges on platforms like Hack The Box, OverTheWire, and picoCTF to apply and reinforce your skills.
- **Categories**: Explore various categories within CTF challenges, including binary exploitation, reverse engineering, and cryptography.

Read Relevant Books and Resources:

- **Reverse Engineering Books**: Consult authoritative books on reverse engineering, such as "Practical Reverse Engineering" by Bruce Dang, et al., and "The IDA Pro Book" by Chris Eagle.
- **Online Resources**: Leverage online platforms, blogs, and forums for continuous learning and updates on new techniques.

Take Online Courses and Training:

- **Online Platforms**: Enroll in online courses on platforms like Coursera, Udacity, or edX that offer specialized training in reverse engineering.
- **Certifications**: Consider pursuing certifications like OSCP (Offensive Security Certified Professional) or CISSP (Certified Information Systems Security Professional) to validate your skills.

Contribute to Open Source Projects:

- **GitHub**: Contribute to open source reverse engineering projects on platforms like GitHub to collaborate with the community and gain practical experience.
- **Review Code**: Analyze and review code written by experienced reverse engineers to enhance your understanding.

Stay Informed on Industry Trends:

- **Conferences and Workshops**: Attend conferences such as DEF CON, Black Hat, and REcon to stay updated on the latest trends, tools, and research in reverse engineering.
- **Webinars and Talks**: Participate in webinars and talks hosted by experts in the field for insights into advanced techniques and real-world applications.

Build a Network and Seek Mentorship:

- **Online Forums**: Join online forums and communities such as Reddit's r/ReverseEngineering to connect with fellow enthusiasts and experts.
- **Networking Events**: Attend local or virtual networking events to build relationships with professionals in the field.

- **Mentorship**: Seek mentorship from experienced reverse engineers who can provide guidance and share their insights.

Practice Continuous Learning:

- **Stay Curious**: Develop a mindset of curiosity and a willingness to explore new challenges.
- **Continuous Challenges**: Engage in continuous learning by taking on progressively challenging reverse engineering tasks and projects.

By following these steps, aspiring reverse engineers can build a strong foundation of skills and expertise, allowing them to navigate the complexities of analyzing software and hardware systems effectively. Continuous learning, hands-on practice, and active participation in the reverse engineering community are key elements in the journey toward becoming a proficient reverse engineer.

14.2 Job Opportunities and Industries for Reverse Engineers

Reverse engineers play a crucial role in various industries, contributing to cybersecurity, software development, and innovation. Here are some job opportunities and industries where reverse engineers are in high demand:

Cybersecurity Analyst:

- **Responsibilities**: Analyzing malware, identifying vulnerabilities, and developing security solutions.
- **Skills**: Proficiency in reverse engineering tools, malware analysis, and understanding of cybersecurity concepts.

Security Researcher:

- **Responsibilities**: Conducting research on emerging threats, vulnerabilities, and exploitation techniques.
- **Skills**: In-depth knowledge of reverse engineering, vulnerability analysis, and expertise in identifying security issues.

Penetration Tester (Ethical Hacker):

- **Responsibilities**: Assessing the security of systems, networks, and applications to identify and mitigate vulnerabilities.
- **Skills**: Reverse engineering skills for analyzing potential attack vectors, understanding exploits, and recommending security improvements.

Incident Responder:

- **Responsibilities**: Investigating and responding to security incidents, including analyzing malicious activities and developing response strategies.
- **Skills**: Malware analysis, reverse engineering, and the ability to understand and mitigate security incidents.

Software Engineer (Security-Focused):

- **Responsibilities**: Developing secure software, identifying and fixing vulnerabilities, and implementing security best practices.
- **Skills**: Understanding of secure coding practices, vulnerability analysis, and reverse engineering for debugging and code improvement.

Forensic Analyst:

- **Responsibilities**: Examining digital evidence, analyzing malware, and conducting forensic investigations.
- **Skills**: Proficiency in reverse engineering, malware analysis, and forensic tools for investigating cybercrimes.

Threat Intelligence Analyst:

- **Responsibilities**: Monitoring and analyzing threat landscapes, identifying trends, and providing actionable intelligence to improve security posture.
- **Skills**: Reverse engineering capabilities for understanding and profiling threats, as well as contributing to threat intelligence databases.

Embedded Systems Engineer:

- **Responsibilities**: Analyzing and developing solutions for embedded systems, IoT devices, and firmware.
- **Skills**: Expertise in hardware-level reverse engineering, firmware analysis, and understanding of embedded systems.

Digital Rights Management (DRM) Analyst:

- **Responsibilities**: Analyzing and assessing digital rights protection mechanisms in software, games, and media.
- **Skills**: Reverse engineering skills for understanding and circumventing DRM protections.

Malware Analyst:

- **Responsibilities**: Analyzing and dissecting malware to understand its functionality, behavior, and potential impact.
- **Skills**: Proficiency in dynamic and static analysis techniques, reverse engineering tools, and malware behavior analysis.

Intellectual Property Protection Specialist:

- **Responsibilities**: Protecting intellectual property by analyzing and preventing unauthorized use or replication.
- **Skills**: Understanding of reverse engineering for identifying and addressing potential threats to intellectual property.

Consultant/Advisor:

- **Responsibilities**: Providing expert advice on security, vulnerability assessment, and risk mitigation to organizations.
- **Skills**: Diverse knowledge in reverse engineering, cybersecurity, and the ability to offer strategic guidance.

Industries:

Cybersecurity Companies:

- **Roles**: Cybersecurity Analyst, Security Researcher, Penetration Tester.
- **Demand**: High demand for professionals who can assess and improve the security posture of organizations.

Software Development and IT Companies:

- **Roles**: Security-Focused Software Engineer, Incident Responder.
- **Demand**: Increasing focus on secure coding practices and addressing vulnerabilities in software products.

Law Enforcement and Government Agencies:

- **Roles**: Forensic Analyst, Threat Intelligence Analyst.

- **Demand**: Growing need for experts to investigate cybercrimes, analyze threats, and respond to security incidents.

Embedded Systems and IoT Industry:

- **Roles**: Embedded Systems Engineer.
- **Demand**: Rising demand for experts who can analyze and secure embedded systems, IoT devices, and firmware.

Media and Entertainment Industry:

Roles: DRM Analyst.

Demand: Protection of digital content through DRM solutions requires experts in reverse engineering.

Consulting Firms:

Roles: Consultant/Advisor.

Demand: Consulting firms seek professionals who can provide specialized expertise in cybersecurity and reverse engineering.

Financial Institutions:

Roles: Cybersecurity Analyst, Penetration Tester.

Demand: Financial institutions prioritize security to protect sensitive financial information from cyber threats.

Healthcare Industry:

Roles: Security Researcher, Incident Responder.

Demand: Increasing focus on securing healthcare systems and protecting patient data from cyber threats.

Gaming Industry:

Roles: Security Researcher, DRM Analyst.

Demand: Protection of gaming software and prevention of unauthorized access are critical in the gaming industry.

Technology Research and Development Labs:

Roles: Security Researcher, Reverse Engineer.

Demand: Research labs require experts in reverse engineering to explore and develop cutting-edge technologies.

As technology continues to advance, the demand for skilled reverse engineers is expected to grow across various industries. Professionals with expertise in analyzing and securing complex systems will play a vital role in safeguarding digital assets and mitigating cybersecurity risks.

14.3 Continuous Learning and Professional Development

Continuous learning and professional development are essential for staying at the forefront of reverse engineering, given the rapidly evolving nature of technology and cybersecurity. Here are strategies and recommendations for professionals to enhance their skills and knowledge over time:

Stay Informed on Industry Trends:

- **Follow Blogs and Forums**: Regularly read blogs, forums, and online communities related to reverse engineering to stay updated on the latest tools, techniques, and research.
- **Subscribe to Newsletters**: Subscribe to newsletters from reputable cybersecurity organizations and industry experts for curated updates.

Attend Conferences and Workshops:

- **Participate in Industry Events**: Attend conferences such as DEF CON, Black Hat, and REcon to gain insights into emerging trends, network with experts, and attend workshops.
- **Virtual Events**: Explore virtual conferences and webinars, especially when physical attendance is not feasible.

Enroll in Online Courses:

- **Platforms and MOOCs:** Utilize online learning platforms, massive open online courses (MOOCs), and educational resources dedicated to reverse engineering.
- **Certifications**: Consider pursuing certifications from reputable organizations to validate your skills, such as OSCP (Offensive Security Certified Professional) or GREM (GIAC Reverse Engineering Malware).

Participate in Capture The Flag (CTF) Challenges:

- **Join CTF Platforms**: Engage in Capture The Flag challenges on platforms like Hack The Box, OverTheWire, and picoCTF to apply and reinforce your reverse engineering skills.
- **Compete in CTF Competitions**: Participate in CTF competitions, both individually and as part of a team, to challenge yourself with diverse scenarios.

Contribute to Open Source Projects:

- **GitHub Contributions**: Contribute to open source reverse engineering projects on platforms like GitHub to collaborate with the community and gain practical experience.
- **Review Code:** Analyze and review code written by experienced reverse engineers to enhance your understanding.

Engage in Continuous Challenges:

- **Progressive Skill Building**: Take on progressively challenging reverse engineering tasks and projects to build and refine your skills.
- **Hackathons and Challenges**: Participate in hackathons and online challenges that focus on reverse engineering to test your abilities in real-world scenarios.

Join Professional Associations:

- **Network with Peers**: Join professional associations related to cybersecurity and reverse engineering to network with peers and gain insights from experienced professionals.
- **Local Meetups**: Attend local or virtual meetups to connect with professionals in your area and discuss industry trends.

Read Research Papers and Publications:

- **Academic Journals**: Explore academic journals, research papers, and publications related to reverse engineering to deepen your understanding of theoretical concepts.
- **Conference Papers**: Review papers presented at conferences to stay informed about cutting-edge research in the field.

Mentorship and Knowledge Sharing:

- **Seek Mentorship**: Seek mentorship from experienced reverse engineers who can provide guidance, share their experiences, and offer advice on career development.
- **Share Knowledge**: Contribute to knowledge-sharing within the community by sharing your experiences, insights, and expertise through blog posts, tutorials, or presentations.

Build a Personal Lab:

- **Hands-On Practice**: Set up a personal lab environment to practice and experiment with different reverse engineering scenarios.
- **Simulate Real-world Conditions**: Create environments that simulate real-world conditions, allowing you to apply your skills in practical situations.

Explore Emerging Technologies:

- **Stay Curious**: Develop a mindset of curiosity and explore emerging technologies such as machine learning, blockchain, and IoT to understand their implications for reverse engineering.
- **Experiment and Innovate**: Experiment with integrating new technologies into your reverse engineering projects and explore innovative approaches to analysis.

Cross-disciplinary Learning:

- **Interdisciplinary Courses**: Explore courses and resources that bridge reverse engineering with related fields such as cryptography, machine learning, and hardware security.
- **Expand Skill Set**: Broaden your skill set to become a versatile professional capable of addressing diverse challenges.

Attend Webinars and Talks:

- **Industry Webinars**: Participate in webinars hosted by industry experts and organizations to gain insights into advanced techniques, case studies, and best practices.
- **Online Lectures**: Explore online lectures and talks that cover a wide range of reverse engineering topics.

Document Your Learning Journey:

- **Maintain a Learning Journal**: Document your learning journey, challenges faced, solutions found, and key takeaways to reflect on your progress.
- **Portfolio Development**: Create a portfolio showcasing your projects, achievements, and contributions to demonstrate your expertise to potential employers.

By adopting a mindset of continuous learning, staying engaged with the community, and actively seeking out opportunities for skill development, reverse engineers can not only keep pace with industry advancements but also contribute to the growth and innovation within the field.

As we reach the final page of "**The Art of Breaking**," it's time to reflect on the vast landscape of knowledge you've traversed in the world of reverse engineering. Throughout this journey, you've explored the fundamentals of binary analysis, dissected software protections, delved into the intricacies of malware, and ventured into the realms of hardware and network protocol reverse engineering.

The art you've mastered extends beyond the technical skills acquired—it encompasses a mindset, a way of thinking that embraces challenges and thrives on unraveling complexity. You've become adept at using tools like IDA Pro and Ghidra, creating a personalized reverse engineering environment, and choosing the right approach for different tasks.

This book has not only provided you with practical insights but also presented ethical considerations essential in the ever-evolving landscape of technology. As you turn the final page, remember that the power bestowed upon you by this knowledge comes with great responsibility. The legal and ethical aspects of reverse engineering, explored in depth, serve as a compass to navigate the intricate paths of this discipline.

We've examined case studies, drawing lessons from real-world examples, and glimpsed into the future of reverse engineering—embracing emerging technologies, acknowledging challenges, and anticipating opportunities. The conclusion is not an endpoint but a launchpad for your continued exploration.

Whether you're a seasoned professional or an aspiring enthusiast, this book serves as a foundation upon which you can build a fulfilling career in reverse engineering. The world of opportunities awaits, and the skills you've honed can unlock doors across various industries.

As you close this chapter, remember that mastering the art of breaking is not just about breaking things—it's about understanding, innovating, and contributing to a world where knowledge is the key to progress. The journey doesn't end here; it's a perpetual exploration of the ever-expanding frontiers in the captivating realm of reverse engineering.

Thank you for joining us on this adventure. May your curiosity continue to thrive, your skills continue to evolve, and your contributions shape the future of technology.